Le Saulchoir On Trial

Étienne Fouilloux

Unam Sanctam Series 1

Unam Sanctam is a book series devoted to the brilliant generation of Catholic thinkers who inspired a renaissance in twentieth-century Catholic theology and made a decisive contribution at the Second Vatican Council. The principal figures were predominantly though not exclusively French-speaking and included leading Dominicans and Jesuits who contributed to what became known as the *nouvelle théologie*. By retrieving the biblical, patristic and medieval riches of the Catholic tradition (*ressourcement*), the movement sought to reform and to revitalise the Church, to promote a richer evangelisation, and to enable a more effective redemptive engagement with the contemporary world (*aggiornamento*). International in scope, the series will offer new editions and translations of texts as well as studies that examine the history of the *nouvelle théologie*, its exponents, supporters, and opponents. It will also publish works attempting to do for the present age what the *ressourcement theologians* did for their time.

Series Editors

Gabriel Flynn, Dublin City University, Ireland
Joseph A. Komonchak, Professor Emeritus of Theology and Religious Studies, The Catholic University of America, USA
Étienne Fouilloux, Professor Emeritus and Honorary Professor of Lumière University Lyon, France.

Le Saulchoir On Trial

(1932–1943)

Étienne Fouilloux

Translated by Patricia Kelly

Adelaide
2022

ISBN: 978-1-922737-59-5   Soft
978-1-922737-60-1   Hardback
978-1-922737-61-8   Epub
978-1-922737-62-5   Pdf

Published and edited by

Making a lasting impact
An imprint of the ATF Press Publishing Group
owned by ATF (Australia) Ltd.
PO Box 234
Brompton, SA 5007
Australia
ABN 90 116 359 963
www.atfpress.com

Table of Contents

Introduction

February 1942. The world is on fire and bloody. The United States has just entered the war following the aggressive attack on their air and naval base at Pearl Harbour at the beginning of December. The German troops besiege Leningrad and are fighting before Moscow. The Wannsee Conference of 20 January has just established the logistics of the 'final solution' for Jews under the ascendancy of the Third Reich. The Japanese seize Singapore on 15 February . . . No one seems capable of stopping the destructive march of the totalitarian regimes. At the Vatican, however, proceedings follow their course as if nothing was any different: a decree of the Holy Office places on the Index of Prohibited Books two works concerning the definition of theology, outsiders to the noise and violence of a war henceforth worldwide: the *Essai sur le problème théologique* [Essay on the theological problem] by the Belgian Dominican Louis Charlier, published in 1938, and the small booklet *Une école de théologie: le Saulchoir* [A school of theology: the Saulchoir], by his French colleague Marie-Dominique Chenu, published privately at the end of the previous year.

The unfathomable distance between the sanction and its context can only interrogate the historian for answers: modest in its size, style and distribution, *Une école de théologie* was nevertheless one of the rare theological productions in the French language punishable by the Index after the modernist crisis[1]. If a certain number of publications had some problems with Roman censorship, according to the usual euphemism, one could count on two hands those who had undergone the maximal penalty: besides *Une école de théologie* and the *Essai* by his companion in misfortune, Louis Charlier, only *Les événements et la foi* [Events and faith] of the movement 'Jeunesse de l'Église' [Youth of the Church], in 1953, and four works by the philosopher Henry Duméry, in 1958, suffered a similar misfortune; but not *Surnatural* [Supernatural] by the Jesuit Henri de Lubac, nor *Le Phénomène humaine* [The Phenomenon of Man] by his colleague and friend Pierre Teilhard de Chardin, nevertheless quite threatened[2]. The disproportion

---

1. Already condemned during this period, the philosopher Édouard le Roy and the theologian Lucien Laberthonnière were once again sanctioned, in 1931 for the former, and in 1937 and 1941 for posthumous writings of the latter.

2. To these can be added the thesis of the Abbot Marc Oraison, *Vie chrétienne et problèmes de la sexualité* [Christian life and problems of sexuality], decree of 18 March 1953 published only in January 1955 (Agnès Desmazières, « La psychanalyse entre médiatisation et censure. La morale sexuelle de Marc Oraison en procès, 1955-1966 », *Archives de sciences sociales des religions* (juillet-décembre 2013): 123--131. On all these aspects, Étienne Fouilloux, *Une Église en quête de liberté. La pensée catholique française entre modernisme et Vatican II, 1914-1962* (Paris, Desclée de Brouwer, 2006 2ᵉ édition); and « Affaires françaises, archives romaines. Les dossiers du Saint-Office (1920–1938) », *Revue suisse d'histoire religieuse et culturelle*, 107 (2013): 193–204.

between the slimness of the pamphlet by Fr Chenu and the severity of the measures imposed on it, especially at the time when the sanction applied, remains an enigma. What did it contain that was so explosive to merit such a serious sanction? Unlike Charlier's book, it was not the subject of any public discussion having hardly been available except in very small numbers at the end of 1937 and the beginning of 1938 . . . The question aroused much conjecture at the time. As often in similar cases, the condemnation endowed *Une école de théologie* with a coverage quite above the one that it could reasonably have hoped for in normal distribution. The reissue of the pamphlet, in Italy then in France, and the opening of the Dominican archives, have allowed a period of forty years to shed some light on an episode that has become symbolic of the fate of theological research in the Catholic Church on the eve of Vatican II[3].

---

3. *Le Saulchoir. Una scuola di teologia*, Introduction by Giuseppe Alberigo (Casale Monferrato: Marietti, 1982), 110; *Une école de théologie: le Saulchoir*, with studies by Giuseppe Alberigo, Étienne Fouilloux, Jean Ladrière and Jean-Pierre Jossua (Paris: Cerf, 1985), 178 [forthcoming English translation by ATF Press); then Emilio Panella, « Due maestri in una scuola di teologia: Cordovani e Chenu », in *Vita sociale* XL (1983): 166–176; and « Come fu condannata "Una scuola di teologia" di Chenu », in *Vita sociale* XLII (1985): 268–281; Andrea Riccardi, « Une école de théologie fra la Francia e Roma », *Cristianesimo nella storia*, 5 (1985): 11–28; Robert Guelluy, « Les antécédents de l'encyclique 'Humani generis' dans les sanctions romaines de 1942: Chenu, Charlier, Draguet », in *Revue d'Histoire ecclésiastique*, (1986): 421–497; Dominique Avon, *Les Frères prêcheurs en Orient. Les dominicains du Caire (années 1920-années 1960)* (Paris: Cerf, 2005), 342–350; and more recently, Ward De Pril, *Theological Renewal and the Resurgence of Integrism. The René Draguet Case (1942) in its Context* (Leuven: Peeters, 2016), 334.

After two previous essays,[4] reliant on the sources then available, we take up the affair again in the following pages. In a systematic way, with all the accessible documents on this side of the Alps, papers of Fr Chenu and archives of the Dominican province of France, that is to say Paris, notably, without waiting for the opening of the archives of the Holy Office which alone will provide the final word[5]. Who denounced *Une école de théologie*? Who investigated the prosecution case? Was there internal debate at the Supreme Sacred Congregation of the Holy Office over the case? Was Pius XII content to endorse the decision or did he leave his own mark? These questions will only find an answer in Rome, as evidenced by an earlier, and unrecognised, prosecution case concerning the Saulchoir. The article that has been taken from it is resumed here as a preface to the affair of 1942–1943. The available sources before the opening of the Pius XII collection already allowed the acquisition of a pretty clear vision of the origins, context and unfolding of the crisis, if not of its conclusion.

Now accessible to researchers, the Charlier and Chenu files in the Holy Office allow us to respond to some longstanding questions. One of the appointed consultors, Mgr Pietro Parente, hitched Chenu and Le Saulchoir in a rather circumstantial way to a denunciation of Charlier, in which they were not mentioned. A 'relazione' of the

---

4. Étienne Fouilloux, « Le Saulchoir en procès (1937-1942) », *Une école de théologie: le Saulchoir*, 1985, 36–59; and « Autour d'une mise à l'Index », *Marie-Dominique Chenu Moyen-Âge et modernité* (Paris: Centre d'études du Saulchoir/Cerf, 1997), 25–56.

5. The documents without reference come from the papers of Chenu, held in the Archives of the Dominican Province of France (ADF).

whole was then requested from Fr Garrigou-Lagrange. This is the only document which incriminates Chenu in either file, and it played a major role in his being placed on the Index alongside Charlier.[6]

---

6. Archives of the Congregation of the Doctrine of the Faith, 'Censura librorum', 101/1941 (Charlier), 472/1955 (Chenu).

Chapter I
The Saulchoir Denounced (1932)

The affair concerning the house of studies of the Dominican province of France, which begins in 1937 with the quite modest publication of *Une école de théologie: le Saulchoir*, a syllabus pamphlet by its regent Fr Marie-Dominique Chenu, and concludes in 1942 with its placement on the Index and with the eviction from the Saulchoir of its author, has not yet yielded all its secrets[1]. The archives of the Congregation of the Holy Office, a short while ago opened for the pontificate of Pius XI, reveal that the affair was preceded by a first alert in 1932, unknown to the principal parties and therefore to Dominican collective memory[2].

1. Text previously appearing in the *Revue des sciences philosophiques et théologiques* (from now on *RSPT*) (Paris: Librarie philosophique Vrin, 96, 2012), 93-105, under the title 'First alert on the Saulchoir (1932)'.
2. Under the title « L'insegnamento di alcuni Professori del Saulchoir nel 1932 », file Prot. 1463/1932, Rerum variarum 1932 n° 32, Archives of the Congregation for the Doctrine of the Faith, Holy Office. Except where indicated, all documents cited are from this file.

1. A Serious Calling into Question

On 2 May 1932, the day after the turbulent visit to the Saulchoir of the provincial Jourdain Padé, two student brothers, Dalmace (Gérard) Besançon[3] and André (Marie-Madeleine) Bonduelle,[4] sent to the Pope a handwritten document of 124 pages that they themselves present as a denunciation while at the same time requesting anonymity: 'if one knew there was denunciation and

---

3. Born on 7 April 1902 at Provenchères-sur-Meuse (Meuse), student at the Séminaire français de Rome (1919–1925), doctor of philosophy and of theology, he was ordained priest at Langres on 11 June 1925 before entering the Order in 1928. He made simple profession there on 12 November 1929 but had to renounce final profession in 1932; holder of various posts in the diocese of Langres, he was unsuccessful again in religious life in 1949–1950: with the Bénédictines de la Source, in Paris, then in the Dominican Province of Toulouse. He ended his priestly life in the diocese of Troyes and died in 1958 (information provided by the chancellery of Langres and by the Séminaire français de Rome); henceforth reference entry by Tangi Cavalin in the *Dictionnaire biographique des frères prêcheurs* (online).

4. Born on 20 April 1901 at Marquette-lez-Lille (Nord), he completed his priestly studies at the major seminary and at the university seminary of Lille as well as at the French seminary Rome (1927–1928); he was ordained priest at Lille on 8 July 1928. Nephew on his mother's side of Fr Thomas Dehau, he entered the Order in 1929, made his simple profession in 1930 and his solemn profession in 1933. After his captivity in Germany from 1940 to 1945, he founded the Dominican house at Helsinki in 1949 and died after his ultimate return to France on 15 January 1980 (information provided by Br Jean-Michel Potin, archivist of the Dominican province of France, whose help we gratefully acknowledge).

that this denunciation came from us, the conditions of religious and fraternal life would become difficult for us', they wrote humbly in their cover letter.[5] The procedure showed nothing out of the ordinary: in its canon 1397 of the Code of Canon Law 1917, does it not make it a duty 'to all the faithful, above all to clerics, to those who are of ecclesiastical rank and to persons of distinguished standing, to defer to the local bishops or to the Holy See the books which will have been judged harmful'? From publications to teachings on which they can lean is easy to cover. Also, the history of Catholic thought from the early twentieth century rings of rumours of denunciation, as numerous as difficult to prove. By chance, if one can say so, the historian is dealing here with a denunciation in due and good form. The blow comes from two former students from the French Seminary of Rome, a well-known home of antimodernism up until the eviction in 1922 of its superior, the spiritan Henri Le Floch. One of them at least, the Abbot Besançon, became known there as an ardent propagandist of the theses of Charles Maurras.[6] Both entered the Dominican Order after having been ordained priests, for the diocese of Langres (Besançon), for the diocese of Lille (Bonduelle). Students of third- and second-year theology at the Saulchoir in 1931–1932, they have not yet made their final profession.

The document addressed to Pius XI consisted of two large parts: thirty pages on 'The general spirit of the Saulchoir',[7] attributable to Besançon, who seems the

---

5. Evidence no. 1 of the file.

6. Information communicated by Paul Airiau, author of an unpublished reference thesis *Le Séminaire français de Rome du P. Le Floch, 1904-1927* (Paris: Institut d'études politiques, 2003).

7. Evidence no. 7.

principal instigator of the process; and ninety-four pages on the teaching of four of the lecturers at the studium: Paul Synave and Ceslas Spicq, teachers of Holy Scripture; Marie-Dominique Chenu and Antonin-Dalmace Sertillanges, teachers of philosophy and theology. 'We believe we recognize in the spirit that reigns here, in the doctrines that the majority of our Lector Priests profess, a spirit and doctrines very close to those denounced and condemned by Pope Pius X in his encyclical *Pascendi*,[8] write the two complainants. They recognise certainly that with its 85 Dominican students, to which are added those of the Fathers of La Salette and the Barnabites, the Salicetin convent is 'flourishing'. And that all its masters are not contaminated by the spirit that they denounce: Fr Vincent Héris, regent of studies since 1928, in particular escaped it; but he would be under the influence of his assistant Paul Synave. Despite this exception, 'the tendencies and the doctrines of almost all the Lector Fathers seem to us tainted with a remainder or a revival of modernism', assert Besançon and Bonduelle.[9] The accusation is extremely serious: a quarter of a century after the condemnation of modernism, which Pius X defined as the 'meeting (place) of all heresies', the antimodernist suppression continues to find victims in the bosom of the Catholic Church: four works by the philosopher Édouard Le Roy, successor of his master Henri Bergson at the Collège de France, were put on the Index in 1931.[10]

---

8. Letter cited on 2 May 1932.
9. Letter cited on 2 May 1932. In the Dominican vocabulary, the assistantship in theology gives access to the teaching body.
10. Decree of 27 June, published in the *Acta Apostolicae Sedis* of 5 August, 330.

For Besançon, no doubt at all: the spirit of the house of studies 'strangely resembles, alas, the one described by Pius X in his description of modernism'.[11] And he lists three proofs of this which he considers to be convincing in his view. First, 'a certain self-importance' that would lead notably to a lack of 'respect for the authority of Roman congregations'. Then and especially 'a great love for all novelties', preferably 'advanced', and in particular 'for modernism and the current modernists': 'M. Bergson is highly favoured' by Fr Sertillanges and 'the condemnation of M. Leroy [*sic*] has been rather badly received'.[12] Finally, a great laxity in the field of moral doctrine: 'the general spirit is a "broad spirit", a spirit of concession even on the laws of Christ'.[13] Extracts from two theses read in front of teachers without them reacting is proof. 'The notion of dogma proposed by M. Le Roy contains elements of truth that the authentic notion of dogmatic truth can encompass', one would read in the first thesis, presented on 22 January 1932 in front of Héris, Chenu and Spicq.[14] 'The dogma of the Immaculate Conception is a typical example of the dogmatic evolution under the influence of religious sentiment', one would read in the second thesis, to which Frs Synave, Chenu and Spicq did not make the slightest reproach on 8 April 1932.[15] The second assertion, perfectly defendable from the point of view of the historian, falls under the accusation of relativism, and the first would not take the slightest account of the banning of the position of the philosopher on the nature

---

11. 'The General Spirit of the Saulchoir', 1.

12. 'The General Spirit of the Saulchoir', 6.

13. 'The General Spirit of the Saulchoir', 13.

14. 'The General Spirit of the Saulchoir', 17–30.

15. 'The General Spirit of the Saulchoir', 13–16.

of dogma, in proposition 26 of the decree of the Holy
Office *Lamentabili*, on 3 July 1907.

The teachings of the four lecturers that would have 'the
most influence' take up the second part of the report. On
Synave and Spicq, the two signatories consider themselves
'objective', as they confirm relying on notes taken down of
what was dictated in class.[16] The nineteen pages devoted
to Fr Synave pin his conception of biblical inspiration,
and exegesis in general, that would be 'in opposition with
pontifical documents' to the Pentateuch or the Gospel
of John. 'Finally, it must be said—not only did Rev Fr
Synave's course contain *absolutely nothing* which could
benefit from Holy Scripture from a spiritual point of view,
nothing that could further piety—but the atmosphere
of this course is a mind-deadening atmosphere. We are
always in contact with Protestants, with rationalists. It is
only "science" that matters and counts.'[17] Regarding the
introduction to the Bible course by Fr Spicq, Bonduelle
is no gentler. A plethora of citations serves to prove that
his literary critique of the Bible shatters its authenticity
as does his unwavering criticism of exactitude.[18] If the
name of Fr Marie-Joseph Lagrange, founder of the École
biblique de Jérusalem, is not cited by the two accusers, it
is his approach to scriptural texts that seems targeted. Fr
Synave spent a year in Jerusalem in 1913–1914 and he
did not use the historico-critical method on the biblical
writings covered: indeed, he plays an important role at
the Institute of Medieval Studies of the Saulchoir where
the same method was applied to the writings of St Thomas
Aquinas. As for his student Fr Spicq, he made a trip to
Jerusalem in 1930. For the record, as his subsequent

---

16. Letter of 2 May.

17. Evidence no. 2, 18-19.

18. Evidence no. 6, 74-94.

evolution would not lead him particularly into laxity, let us add that attached to the dossier was his article 'New reflections on biblical theology', published in the journal of the Saulchoir in 1958![19] The Holy Office, and the Congregation for the Doctrine of the Faith following, proceeded by accumulation: nothing is lost, everything is preserved.

The two signatories are a deal less sure of themselves regarding the teachings of Sertillanges and Chenu. Impossible to be as precise about the former, as neither student took notes in his classes. Sertillanges, assigned since 1928 to the Saulchoir after his retirement in 1922 from the Catholic Institute of Paris, where he taught philosophy, and his exile in Jerusalem and then in the Netherlands, attributed therefore, either to the accusations of agnosticism to which he was the subject at the height of the modernist crisis, or to his public opposition to the note of Benedict XV on peace in 1917,[20] he would enjoy true reverence in the house and would contribute 'for a great deal to what one calls here "the spirit of the Saulchoir".[21] Besides his weakness for Bergson, Besançon pins his supposed opposition to the encyclical *Pascendi* as far as the evolution of dogma and apologetics are concerned; and to social encyclicals or to the letter on the Le Sillon movement as far as 'human dignity' and relationships between the Church and society are concerned.

---

19. *RSPT*, 42 (1958): 209–219.

20. Today one knows that this retirement and this exile were due to serious personal breaches in the context of the *Revue des jeunes*: see Anne Simonin, *Les Éditions de Minuit, 1942–1955. Le devoir d'insoumission*, IMEC Éditions, 1994, 37–43 (on the religious path of Pierre de Lescure, spiritual son of Sertillanges and editorial secretary of the journal).

21. Evidence no. 3, 20–39 (citation, 20).

As for Fr Chenu, his thought is 'elusive and obscure'.[22] We will know no more about it: the pages on his case are missing from the 1932 file.[23] In all likelihood they only concerned his courses, and notably his famous 'introduction to the history of Christian doctrines'.[24] But his censors would have found grain to grind in a recent article in *La Vie intellectuelle*, the journal of his Juvisy colleagues: 'The meaning and the lessons of a religious crisis'. Under the pretext of a compilation of the first serious study on the modernist crisis, that of the Abbot Jean Rivière,[25] Fr Chenu reduced the episode to 'a normal effect of intellectual growth in Christian society'. The 'condemnation of modernism was only, according to him, the necessary condition and the negative aspect of a progress in which today we measure extreme interest, and from which profit is still to be made. The error irrevocably eliminated, in its principles, in its methods, in its results, charity emanated from solid work whereby its value was concealed for a time and almost compromised soundness.' This 'robust optimism' prevents locking oneself 'in a scholarly Thomism, hardened by centuries-old generations of textbooks and unhinged by the intrusion of a massive dose of "baroque" theology', which confines itself 'to basic condemnations, through ignorance of the very position of the questions' and suffers

---

22. Letter of 2 May.

23. Where they covered, under numbers 4 and 5, pages 40 to 73.

24. 'Christianity and Holy Empire' and 'The Aristotelianism of Marsilius of Padua' were his two other courses in 1931–1932 (Carmelo Giuseppe Conticello, *De contemplatione* (Angelicum, 1920). Unpublished doctoral thesis of Fr M.-D. Chenu, in *RSPT*, 75 (1991): 421.

25. *Le Modernisme dans l'Église. Étude d'histoire religieuse contemporaine* (Paris: Letouzey et Ané, 1929).

on account of a 'certain positivist intellectualism, making use of Thomism as a paragon of [its] pseudo-religious fundamentalism'. On the contrary, an honest approach to religious philosophy, to biblical exegesis and to the history of dogmas must allow one to overcome the crisis through the elaboration of a higher synthesis.[26] This bold program caused upheavals in Thomistic circles. 'If you knew how much good your article in *La Vie intellectuelle* has done', wrote Étienne Gilson.[27] 'Fr Chenu went to a great deal of effort to write his modest article on modernism. He believes that history of itself is salutary, just as Fr Delos believes sociology to be. They do not understand the role of metaphysics and of theology', regrets on the other hand Abbot Charles Journet, friend and advisor of Jacques Maritain.[28] Such a program had nothing to please the two informers any longer, nourished in Rome by the rigid teaching of Cardinal Billot. But their prose is missing: 'Numbers four and five have been switched to Fr Chenu's position', wrote an anonymous hand on their report: 'position' that has been dedicated to him later when his *École de théologie* was referred to the Holy Office, in all likelihood.[29] As his proceedings mainly took place under the pontificate of Pius XII, this 'position' was not available

26. Fascicle of 15 December 1931, 356–380 (citations on pages 367 and 380).

27. Letter to Chenu of 14 February 1932, in *Revue thomiste*, 55 (2005): 29.

28. Letter to Maritain of 7 January 1932, Journet-Maritain, *Correspondance*, volume II, *1930–1939*, (Fribourg/Paris, Éditions universitaires/Éditions Saint-Paul, 1997), 197.

29. 'I nn. 4 e 5 sono stati trasferiti nella posizione del P. Chenu', for which one gives the classification mark: 475/55/i. The 'position' is the open file when a publication is deferred to the Holy Office: for Fr Chenu, his *École de théologie: Le Saulchoir*, in 1937 or 1938.

for consultation. This piece of information deserves nevertheless to be kept: Fr Chenu's file was not empty at the end of the 1930s, since the Holy Office retained in storage the denunciation of 1932.

2. An Inquiry Without Immediate Follow-On

Far from being thrown in the wastepaper basket, the report is sent to the Holy Office who extract from it a summary of five pages on the four religious 'denounced of modernism'.[30] '*Ex audientia Sanctissimi*', according to the established formula, an enquiry is carried out on 12 May 1932 under secrecy of the Holy Office. Without disclosing from whom the complaint came, the nuncio in Paris Mgr Luigi Maglione, because the matter concerned French religious, and the nuncio in Brussels Mgr Clemente Micara, because the Saulchoir was relocated to Belgium from 1903, both had to make enquiries about them, especially about Sertillanges, already known to the Vatican, but also about Synave. As younger men, Chenu and Spicq still seemed unknown.[31] We notice the speed of the procedure: it was held less than fifteen days after the issuing of the denunciation, which was not transmitted to the personalities solicited.

The file assembled by Maglione consisted of eight responses more or less detailed, of which the interest largely went beyond the event that gave birth to them. Several amongst them make it possible to situate the opinion that certain eminent members of the "great family of Thomists" (Étienne Gilson) of the Saulchoir held by. A single layperson is consulted, but his name is

---

30. Evidence no. 8 of the file, n.d.
31. Evidence no. 9 (audience note) and no. 10, minute of the letter to Maglione of 14 May.

worth recording: it is in fact Jacques Maritain, professor of philosophy at the Catholic Institute of Paris. Two bishops give their opinion: Mgr Gabriel Antoine Rasneur of Tournai, as the Saulchoir is within his jurisdiction,[32] and Mgr Jean-Arthur Chollet, archbishop of Cambrai and former professor of theology at the Catholic Faculties of Lille. Also responding are the Jesuit provincial of Champagne, Xavier Thoyer, former professor of theology at the Enghien scholasticate also in Belgium, and four priest-professors of philosophy or theology from French Catholic institutes: the canons Léon Mahieu and Pierre Tiberghien (Lille), the canon Daniel-Joseph Lallement and the Jesuit priest Adhémar d'Alès (Paris).

Three of these responses are blunt refusals. 'As for me, I have never, so far, heard of the teaching of the Saulchoir put into question', a place he rarely visits, writes the Bishop of Tournai after consultation.[33] Same attitude with the two Jesuits. Fr Thoyer, who received his information from professors in Enghien, did not find 'any precise fact to put forward against the orthodoxy of the teaching in question'.[34] Fr d'Alès, dean of the faculty of theology in Paris, is more precise. 'I do not understand what it is all about', he writes. The modernism according to *Pascendi* seemed unthinkable to him in a Dominican Priory at the beginning of the 1930s, so 'what other modernism' could it be about? 'Or else these facts do not exist, or else they have not been communicated to me', he adds. The recent article by Sertillanges 'Saint Thomas, Man of the Present',[35] seemed to him difficult but interesting. A man

---

32. The Saulchoir is a locality of Kain-la-Tombe, not far from Tournai.
33. Document no. 14/1 (28 May).
34. Document no. 14/6 (24 May).
35. *RSPT*, 19 (1930): 669–678.

who has not forgotten the stir caused by the article on the method of immanence in his *Dictionnaire apologétique de la foi catholique*, due to the brothers Albert and Auguste Valensin, he concludes in as bold a way as Chenu: 'there is a modernism that is corruption; but there is a modernism that is life too short; and the latter is not to be feared.'[36].

Canon Tiberghien returns edified each year from his retreat at the Saulchoir and sings praises of the convent. He notes there 'a great spirit of submission to the Holy See and to the directives given by him. In particular this priory has been completely able to avoid the difficulties that the condemnation of Action Française has caused in other religious settings', notably the studium of the province of Toulouse at Saint-Maximin. The argument carries weight when one knows the importance for the apostolic nuncio Maglione and for Pope Pius XI of such a submission. In the eyes of the professor from Lille, the 'filial faithfulness to the Dominican and Thomist tradition is total at the Saulchoir'.[37] The long reply by his colleague Léon Mahieu, although more nuanced, is convergent with his own: 'it does not seem that one finds modernist infiltrations there', he writes. While underscoring this good reputation of the whole, he 'admits to finding at times quite bold and quite inexact views by Fr Sertillanges and Fr Spicq' on social morality.[38] But these two religious had not been part of the teaching body of the Saulchoir for very long,[39] and therefore it is not them who give the place its tone according to him.[40].

---

36. Document no. 14/5 (30 May).

37. Evidence 14/4 (27 May).

38. Fr Spicq was first assigned to the teaching of social philosophy.

39. Spicq since the end of his studies in 1928 and Sertillanges since 1929.

40. Evidence 14/7 (29 May, 12 pages).

The three other consultations are more critical. Jacques Maritain regrets the departure from the Saulchoir of Fr Réginald Garrigou-Lagrange for Rome, in 1909, with whom he was very close. As a result, the axis of the house of studies moved towards history and a conception 'of science as "secularized"', opening into a spirit he judged to be 'scientistic'. In convergence with the denunciation whose letter he ignores he notes there 'a kind of sterility, a certain self-importance, a propensity to flatter the adversary' which moreover extends beyond the Saulchoir to contaminate in his eyes the Dominican province of France as a whole: the philosopher attacks in the same manner the *Documents de la Vie intellectuelle* which juxtapose opposing positions; and also Fr Sertillanges who 'blurs fundamental oppositions and favours the confusion of minds', adds Maritain. But these divergences 'concern more the spirit than doctrine' and more than faith, and there is nothing more to repeat about them. The philosopher however puts his hopes in a new Dominican generation which attaches less weight to history and more to metaphysics.[41] Such an appreciation, measured, of the gap between its Thomism and that of the Saulchoir does not surprise. "For the Saulchoir, yes, the courses of Fr Thomas Philippe, but not the others! Pay attention to the pre-existing de-existentiated/de-existing? pseudo-Thomism!', he would write on 20 December 1933 to his follower Yves Simon, keen to publish some teachings from the Saulchoir.[42] He himself momentarily

---

41. Evidence 14/9, n.d., 7 pages.
42. Jacques Maritain-Yves Simon, *Correspondance*, tome 1, *Les années françaises (1927-1940)* (Tours: CLD éditions, 2008), 162.

interrupted his collaboration with *La Vie intellectuelle* as its evolution disappointed him[43].

The response of the canon Lallement, professor in the Faculty of Philosophy at the Catholic University of Paris, is close to that of his colleague Maritain. He also regrets in the spirit of the Saulchoir, 'a predominance of historical preoccupations over dogmatic preoccupations'. In his view, 'the teaching of Holy Scripture is probably the one where the purely historical and critical orientation still persists the most', but he does not mention any name. With the teaching of the history of dogmas, one must also 'lament some negative consequences, at the time of the period when history took precedence over theology, and of the prevailing attitude of Fr Sertillanges'. They lead to a tendency to exonerate convicted authors and to welcome certain recent books put on the Index 'with an unconcealed impatience'. The point of the attack is aimed at Sertillanges to which Lallement also criticises an underestimation of the 'value of our knowledge of God'; the attack could also be aimed at Chenu whose humour is at times irreverent: 'however aside from that I have always heard praise for the Rev Fr Chenu for the seriousness of his interior life', adds Lallement. All in all, his overall impression is clearly positive: he underlines 'the good that is evident in this house, from which we can expect a lot', from the young generation of readers in particular: his protégé Yves Congar or Thomas Philippe. He would be disappointed by the first, who would not waste any time in becoming one of Chenu's lieutenants, but not by the second, who would replace Chenu as regent in 1942. As with Maritain's reply, his response illustrates the

43. Étienne Fouilloux, « Jacques Maritain, le P. Bernadot et la revue *La Vie intellectuelle* », in *Recherches philosophiques,* 3 (2007): 81–104.

clear difference of orientation between the speculative and mystical Thomism of the disciples of John of Saint-Thomas and the historico- doctrinal Thomism of the Saulchoir.[44]

The only plainly unfavourable response of the house of studies is that of Mgr Chollet. Someone 'very knowledgeable' informed him of Sertillanges' penchant for thinkers whose 'dangerous doctrines he did not need to recall', he writes. 'I noticed myself the doctrinal recklessness of the Rev Fr Spicq in some book review. Someone made me aware one day of a review by Fr Chenu on the subject of Nestorius, where the necessary reserves had not been made'. In short, 'the house is slightly the despair of some old Dominicans. Dreadful spirits can be found there', he was recently told by a 'very solid theologian'. Urged by Maglione to reveal his name, Chollet refused to as the information was communicated to him 'in a personal and confidential capacity' by someone seriously ill who 'would not admit that I gave his name'.[45] Precision points to the abbot Albert Michel, successor of Chollet at the Faculty of Theology of Lille and his trusted man, recently forced to leave there soon after the one that he is suspected of having denounced in Rome, the patrologist Gustave Bardy.[46]

In his report of 31 July, the nuncio in Brussels Micara observes that the Saulchoir is little known in Belgium and has never aroused criticism there, an opinion confirmed by the bishop of Tournai, the professor of Holy scripture

---

44. Evidence 14/8 (24 June, 6 pages). On these distinctions, Henry Donneaud, 'Le Saulchoir, une école de théologie?", in *Gregorianum*, 83 (2002), p. 433-449.

45. Evidence 14/2 (4 June) and 14/3 (10 June).

46. He would then devote himself to the completion of the *Dictionnaire de théologie catholique*.

at the major seminary and the rector of the University of Louvain. The rector of the Jesuit scholasticate of Enghien nevertheless expressed reservations about the thought of Fr Sertillanges: 'a certain imprecision of terms'; 'a somewhat pronounced indulgence, at times, towards authors of non-Catholic works'; 'a slight habit of bringing their theses somewhat superficially closer to Catholic doctrine'. But there is nothing modernist in this thought.[47] On 5 September, after seeing again the Benedictine abbot of Clairvaux, he "they remained faithful" at the Saulchoir, but 'a strange mentality' would reign there which consists in 'brushing against the extreme limit, just so as not to fall into condemned doctrines'.[48]

After providing a summary of the votes and a list of publications,[49] Maglione concludes for his part to have the case dismissed on 1 September.[50] Although Sertillanges and Spicq were at times imprudent in moral and social matters, and while Sertillanges was too conciliatory with non-Catholic thinkers and his language was 'sometimes too bold, paradoxical and perilous', one could not attribute to the religious put under examination 'modernist tendencies literally and truly'.[51] For the nuncio in Paris, the reservations of Lallement, of Mahieu and of Maritain are less concerned about the Saulchoir than about *La Vie intellectuelle* and its *Documents*: escaping the control of Fr Marie-Vincent Bernadot their founder, unwell, they abandoned the role assigned to them by Pope Pius XI: 'to fight the demonstrations of Action française on doctrinal

---

47. Evidence 11, 4 pages.
48. Evidence, 15.
49. Amongst which *Les deux sources de la morale et de la religion* of Bergson recently published.
50. Evidence, 13, 8 pages.
51. Evidence, 7.

ground'; and they were wrong to publish, on Bergson in
particular, questionable pages.[52] Maglione also intervened
twice with the Master General of the Dominicans and
former professor of the Saulchoir, Martin-Stanislas Gillet,
so that Bernadot could be reinstalled in his managerial
functions with full powers: the contentious *Documents*
would disappear in October 1932 and *La Vie intellectuelle*
would become fortnightly. The nuncio in Paris would also
invite Sertillanges, through Gillet, for more 'precision in
doctrinal exposition'.[53] He nevertheless concludes that 'the
spirit of the convent of the Saulchoir, in its teachers and
as well as its students, is progressing for the good'.[54] More
favourable than that of Micara, his report was heard: these
two documents are the last pieces of a file in which the
strongest criticisms concern less the house of studies than
the 'Thomism of the apostolate' of Fr Sertillanges and the
publications of Juvisy where he was all-powerful since
1929: close to the Saulchoir, they are however external
to him and we cannot make him bear the responsibility
for them. No follow up was therefore given to the matter.
However, this belongs to the aftermath of the modernist
crisis: the denunciation was immediately followed by an
investigation for suspicion of modernism on the Saulchoir
and on four of its professors; but this enquiry, far from
leading to sanctions, in fact came to nothing. In France
as in Rome, the wind had turned: while the tensions with
Action française and its defenders within the church

---

52. 'Judgments on Bergson' which juxtapose very distant points
of view without examining them critically, (*Documents*, 20
January 1930, 37–72; 20 February 1930, 245–279; 20 June
1930, 541–588).

53. Evidence 13, 8.

54. Evidence 13, 7.

reach their peak, the antimodernist suppression tends to run out.[55]

3. The Saulchoir as an Example

One will have noticed the absence of Dominicans from the file, although their Master General is by right one of the consultants of the Holy Office. If there had been deliberation amongst these entities, the Order would have been warned of the danger. But there was none and the rule which does not allow the intervention of members of the religious family concerned in the investigation of a case on one or several of its members seems to have been respected. Same thing regarding secrecy: Jacques Maritain did not whisper a word of the affair to his Dominican friends nor to his confidant Charles Journet. Also the religious whose teaching was questioned and their superiors, if they had wind of the denunciation and attributed the main responsibility for it to Br Besançon, do not seem to have been aware of the investigation[56]. From which there comes a paradox; while the house of studies is denounced in Rome by two of its students, the Saulchoir receives a brilliant consecration from the Order. When Fr Gillet, Provincial of France, was elected Master General of the Dominican Order in 1929, it was decided that the next General Chapter would be held in a convent in his Province. Thus the Saulchoir received the capitular body from 25 July to 11 August 1932.

---

55. Étienne Fouilloux, *Une Église en quête de liberté. La pensée catholique française entre modernisme et Vatican II, 1914–1962* (Paris: Desclée de Brouwer, 2nd edition, 2006), 68–84.

56. Tangi Cavalin found in the archives of the Province of France some traces of the affair and of the deleterious climate it generated at the Saulchoir.

Even better: on 7 August one of the threatened teachers successfully passes, in front of a jury composed of five members, to be Master in Sacred Theology, a higher grade for a reader in the Order.[57] We let him recount the event. 'It is traditional that at General Chapters a young professor presents himself to be a Master in Sacred Theology, no longer before a University jury, but before the assembly of the members of the General Chapter. The session loses a little of its academic rigour but benefits in terms of decorum. So I was chosen to sacrifice to tradition, says Fr Marie-Dominic Chenu. Five members of the Chapter had to question me on a prepared questionnaire in advance. This all took place in Latin. I spoke Latin fluently, and it all went extremely well. Such that I was nominated Master in Sacred Theology immediately while ordinarily one must teach for 15 years before being awarded this position.'[58] One of his biographers confirms: 'the members of the "definitory" of this Chapter, very favourably impressed by the fluency and brilliance of the candidate, elected him by exclamation and dispensed him from the delay of seven years then imposed by law between the preliminary exam "*ad gradus*" and the "masters" proper.'[59] Four days after a defense which lasted three hours, Fr Gillet handed over to Chenu, who was only twenty-seven years old, the badges of Master of Sacred Theology.[60] But his promotion did not

---

57. On this topic, see the chronicle by Pierre Benoît, student in the fourth and last year of theology, in *L'Année dominicaine* (octobre 1932): 276–280.

58. *Un théologien en liberté. Jacques Duquesne interroge le Père Chenu* (Paris: Le Centurion, 1975), 53–54.

59. Olivier de La Brosse, *Le Père Chenu. La liberté dans la foi* (Paris: Cerf, 1969), 42.

60. Nomination recorded in the Acts of the chapter, pages 46–47.

stop there. In the previous year already, Gillet had refused Bernadot's request for Chenu's services. 'I do not believe that Fr Chenu is the designated man for Juvisy. First he must stay at the Saulchoir, and I fail to understand why we should disrupt the Saulchoir for Juvisy; I know that the young ones at the Saulchoir care above all about Fr Chenu', he wrote to him on 6 April 1931.[61] Chenu did better than staying at the Saulchoir: he is appointed the Regent of Studies of the Province of France in a letter from Gillet on 3 September 1932. On 10 October following, Héris and Synave are also granted their Master in Sacred Theology.[62] Not only did the investigation into the Saulchoir not have negative consequences, but the priory and several of its professors were set as an example for the entire Order.

Gérard Besançon on the other hand, who was assigned to teach theology in Mosul, is the object of a negative vote at the council of lecturers on 28 June 1932 and judges it preferable to renounce a compromised solemn profession: he leaves the Saulchoir in July and returns to his diocese of Langres, where his sympathies for Action française prevent him being given a position of responsibility commensurate with his high intellectual qualification. André Bonduelle will have better luck the following year, before being chosen in 1949 to re-establish the Dominican order in Finland.

---

61. Archives of the Éditions du Cerf.
62. *L'Année dominicaine* (novembre 1932): 323.

Chapter II
Le Saulchior: A Model or a Foil?
(1937–1942)

1. A Manifesto?

This act takes place at Kain-la Tombe, near Tournai in Belgium, at a place called Le Saulchoir, where, in 1903, the French Dominican Province's house of studies had found refuge, having been expelled from Flavigny-sur-Ozerain (Côte d'Or) by Émile Combes' anticlerical government.[1] On 7 March 1936, the feast of St Thomas Aquinas, Marie-Dominique Chenu, Regent of Studies, replaced the usual panegyric with a sketch of a group portrait. Taking as his text a passage he loved from John's Gospel – 'the truth will set you free' – he offered a summary of the intellectual and spiritual experience of the *studium* over the previous thirty years.[2]

---

1. Chapters II and III were previously published as an article in *RSPT* 98 (2014): 261-352.
2. '"Veritas liberabit vos". La Vérité vous rendra libres', 14 photocopied pages, ADF. The title comes from Jn 8.32; *Veritas* is also the Dominican motto.

His audience's enthusiasm, recounted in the house chronicle,[3] led Chenu to deepen and develop his speech, and thus, at the end of 1937,[4] a 130-page booklet with an austere cover, entitled *Une école de théologie: le Saulchoir* appeared. Printed by the Catholic publisher Casterman in Tournai, it was not made available through the usual commercial channels. The Dominican family for whom it had been written took charge of its distribution, restricted by the very small print run, almost certainly fewer than a thousand.[5] The lack of a publicity machine reduced reviews to the minimum, until the author himself intervened to stop them.[6] Many speculative Thomists were quick to consider Chenu's booklet as a manifesto against their way of understanding theology. While its modest cover did not sit well with such an ambition, the same cannot be said of its content, for based on the singular life of the house of studies where he was Regent, Chenu was proposing an understanding of theology and its teaching methods far removed from the then classical canons of the Order of Friars Preacher and beyond.

---

3. 'Today at High Mass, a magnificent programmatic speech from Very Rev Fr Chenu on the theme, the truth will set you free', ADF.

4. *Imprimi potest* from the Provincial, Padé, 9 November, *imprimatur* from the Archdiocese of Paris the following day.

5. Éditions Casterman were unable to provide the figure; in a letter dated 11 October 1983, Chenu himself suggested it was 700 or 800 copies. Sales were handled from Le Saulchoir, from both Kain and Étiolles.

6. Giuseppe Alberigo found only one, published in the *Theologische Revue* 1939: 48–51, written by Friedrich Stegmüller, a professor at Würzburg. Chenu asked Joseph Dopp, editor of the Louvain *Revue néoscolastique* not to publish a review (letter dated 10 June 1938, passed on by Jean Ladrière).

Let us come to the heart of the crime. First, how did it go from being a sermon to a booklet? The 1926 speech contains the main idea, which had already been expressed five years earlier in an article on the Modernist crisis, which had not passed unnoticed.[7] According to Chenu there was a strong analogy between the crisis of the early twentieth century, and that of the thirteenth. Then the Christian faith had been subject to the challenge of dialectic, the internal competence of Greek philosophy; now it was subject to the challenge of historical criticism. Thomas Aquinas, Albert the Great, and so many others, less famous, had tamed the thought of antiquity without concern for the hesitations or sanctions they encountered, and their true disciples should proceed in the same way with modern history and philosophy, if necessary against a Thomism which was closed in on itself and therefore unfaithful to the enterprising spirit of their master. The three conditions of true freedom for a theological approach were first, the return to the medieval texts from which the later, false commentaries often fell short; second, the transposition to these texts of the historical method of Fr Marie-Joseph Lagrange and his École biblique de Jérusalem—a significant point of reference at Le Saulchoir, according to Chenu; and finally, the locating of intellectual work in a spiritual bath which would abolish the chasm between speculation and contemplation, which in his eyes was so damaging.

A close study of Chenu's public and private writings from his arrival at Le Saulchoir in 1920, and particularly from the time he became Regent in 1932, enables us to

---

7. 'Le sens et les leçons d'une crise religieuse', à propos des Mémoires d'Alfred Loisy, in *La Vie intellectuelle* (10 December 1931): 356–380.

restore the transition from sermon to booklet.[8] Chapter II of the booklet, entitled 'Esprit et méthodes' (pages 33–50), continues in a direct line from the 1936 speech, from which it draws a number of key ideas: the links between the two crises, the return to the medieval substrate based on the authority of the university professor Étienne Gilson (quoted on pages 45, 87, 101), the application of the 'historical method', the primacy of the spiritual with, this time, the authority of Jacques Maritain's *Degrés du savoir* (quoted on pages. 43, 89, 91). The first chapter, 'De Saint-Jacques au Saulchoir' (pages 1–34), the final chapter, 'Les études médiévales' (pages 97–105) and the appendix of joint and individual 'Publications' (pages 109–128), which are more descriptive than conceptual, often tally with the annual reports which the Regent sent to his superiors on studies and publications, reports whose point was always the urgency of the return of the house to its home in the Paris region. We can see this in an extract from a letter dated May 1933 to the Master General, Gillet.

The innovative audacity of St Albert and St Thomas remains the *law of nature* (*loi de nature*) in the Order. Alongside regular teaching, at critical moments in particular – and my God, we are living through one of those!—it provides a sharp but calm clear-sightedness in the discrimination of ideas and a new fruitfulness of more profoundly understood traditional principles. We believe that we are living in as serious and as great a time as the Renaissance, when science, philosophy, and humanism

---

8.   André Duval OP, 'Bibliographie du P. Marie-Dominique Chenu (1921–1965)', *Mélanges offerts à M.-D. Chenu* (Paris: Librairie philosophique Vrin, 1967): 9–29; also Maria Luisa Mazzarello, 'Gli scritti del P. Marie-Dominique Chenu, 1963–1979', in *Salesianum*. 42 (1980): 855–66.

escaped Christian thought. We should like, through the grace of the Order, to contribute to the avoidance of a new defeat of Christendom, which would be more serious than that of the first.[9]

More hard-hitting in its private format than in public, this ambition, whose foundation and shape would soon appear exaggerated, prefigured both the 1936 sketch and its development in 1937. At the heart of *Une école de théologie*, chapters III and IV, respectively entitled 'La Théologie' (pages 51–77)[10] and 'La Philosophie' (pages 78–96), are the result of earlier or contemporary work, even down to the expressions used. These are principally the preface to the second edition of Fr Ambroise Gardeil's *Le Donné révélé et la théologie* (1932), the article 'Les yeux de la foi', published in a Canadian journal the same year, and in particular the major article 'Position de la théologie' published in the *Revue des sciences philosophiques et théologiques* in 1935.[11] But even the briefest review or shortest footnote can contain some of the expressions to which *Une école de théologie* owes its incisive nature. Two examples, among many, will suffice. First a review which in 1935 denounced 'the sin of the baroque theology' of the sixteenth and seventeenth centuries; and the critical note, 'Philosophie et spiritualité', contemporary with the publication of the booklet, which ends with a soon-to-be contested definition of theology as a 'spirituality

---

9. 5 typed pages, ADF (quotation from page 2).
10. Translations from Chapter III are taken from Patricia Kelly, *Ressourcement Theology: A Sourcebook* (London: Bloomsbury/T&T Clark, 2021), 15–31.
11. Préface, Juvisy, pages vii–xiv; *Revue dominicaine*, 38 (1932): 653–660; *RSPT*, 24 (1935): 232–257.

which has found rational tools appropriate to its religious experience.[12]

Thus despite its small immediate audience, *Une école de théologie* certainly seems to be the crystallisation not only of personal reflection, but of a collective spiritual and intellectual adventure, in which the house of studies saw itself reflected, even if this were more the case for Marie-Joseph Congar or Henri-Marie Féret than for others. The force of its author's pen also gave it polemical overtones against his will (or not). One by one Chenu picked up 'a negative conservatism' (page 37), metaphysicians who were over-sure of themselves (pp. 43-44), the Thomist 'system' (page 45), outdated manuals (page 45), a Thomism which had become 'orthodoxy' (page 76), and finally, '"baroque" scholasticism' (pages 83–85), at a moment when, despite Eugenio d'Ors' recent plea,[13] the adjective retained its negative connotations in the French mind. And the list goes on.

There are three major themes of *Une école de théologie*, skilfully drawn out by Giuseppe Alberigo in his introduction to the Italian edition.[14] Faithful here to Ambroise Gardeil, Chenu maintained 'the primacy of the revealed data' in his later explanations, without a shadow of doubt. 'The most perfect theological systematisation adds not a jot of light on the gospel truth' (pages 52, 54). How could he later be accused of an evolutionary understanding of revelation, of which his confrere Charlier was also accused? But the living tradition cannot be reduced to simple abstract deductions. 'Not only is

---

12. *RSPT,* 24 (1935): 706; *La Vie spirituelle* (supplément, 1er mai 1937): 70; words repeated in *Une école de théologie*, 75.

13. *Du baroque* (Paris: Gallimard, 1935).

14. 'Cristianesimo come storia e teologia confessante', *Le Saulchoir una scola di teologia*, vii–xxx.

the conservation of dogmas described, results reached, or decisions taken in the past', it played the role of the 'creating principal and inexhaustible source of new life' (page 66). Chenu's reasoning thus shows a dual expansion. On the one hand he defends the data against speculation, while on the other he defends ecclesial experience against any kind of fixedness. To hold the two ideas in tandem is not at all evident, and both positions would be the subject of criticism.

There is room for a Christianisation of the 'historical method' between a Modernism which submits faith to the vagaries of history, and anti-Modernism which denies history any value. An obvious advantage of the historical method lies in the relativisation of theological systems, that is, dogmatic formulas: 'relativism', a term with a whiff of sulphur, appears three times in relation to theological systems (pages 48, 49, 105) and three times more in relation to dogmatic formulas (page 64).[15] Above all, it is better wedded to the very nature of Christian faith, that is, its historical nature, than are logical constructions. 'The theologian, then, works with history. Her data is not the nature of things or their timeless forms, but events, which respond to an *economy*, whose fulfilment is linked to time, just as size is linked to the body, above the order of essences' (page 61). Salvation came into human history, and its path stretches out to the parousia. Already certain tendencies, both secular and religious, of this history represent to those who know how to read them the 'theological "tropes" *in action*' (page 68), a formula which precedes the 'signs of the times' by some thirty years. In 'Christianity at work', which he observed with a passion, Chenu thus elevated the awakening of the masses, specialist Catholic Action, the ecumenical movement, the

---

15. More than once using 'relativity' for Thomist philosophy, 95.

plurality of cultures and missionary expansion, provided it be purged of its 'outdated colonialism' (page 67–68). Shortly after *Une école de théologie* was published, an initial reading of these 'tropes' was published, with the title 'Dimension nouvelle de la chrétienté', symbolically dedicated to the chaplains of the Young Christian Workers, to whom Le Saulchoir had opened its doors.[16]

Nor did Chenu abandon St Thomas Aquinas' properly conceptual endeavour, as he was often accused of. 'We believe, with St Thomas, in theological reason, and in the science of theology.' (page 71). 'We believe in theological science. We even believe in theological systems' (page 73). 'We are Thomists, by reason, and even, we might say by nature, born in St Thomas by our Dominican vocation' (page 75). For Chenu, the Angelic Doctor remained the master of the understanding of faith *par excellence*, and therefore it was necessary to return directly to his work, rather than that of his commentators, and above all to not let him become set in the abstraction of concepts which depended on the culture of his time. In particular, he emphasised the indispensable continuity of prayer and of a theology which needed to become wisdom again, in the sense of the Ancients, so that it would not get lost in speculation. 'We cannot do theology by adding "corollaria pietatis" to abstract theses, cut off from their objective and subjective *data*, but rather in holding firm to the profound unity of the theological order', he stated (page 71–72). While criticising in passing certain 'baroque' authorities such as the eighteenth-century German philosopher Christian Wolff, it was this programme, laid out in an occasional booklet with a tiny print run, which would be seen as a manifesto. Chenu was clearly subordinating philosophy to theology, granting

---

16. *La Vie intellectuelle* (25 December 1937): 325–351.

theology a modest role which was clearly distinguished from the dogma from which, according to him, it drew its reformable formulations. He also pleaded for an inductive approach starting from the personal history of humanity (a theology worthy of the name was 'a spirituality which has found rational tools appropriate to its religious experience') or their shared history (theology as a gathering of 'theological "tropes" *in action*' provided by current events). Such a discussion of methodology ran deliberately counter to a scholastic definition of theology with its speculative and deductive nature.

2. A Man, A place, A Success Story

2.1. Chenu

Marcel Chenu was born in 1895 at Soisy-sur-Seine, in the wider suburbs south of Paris, not far from Étiolles where Le Saulchoir would later settle. His father was a baker who had set up a small mechanic's business.[17] His secondary schooling, right up to the Baccalauréat, took place at the Catholic Notre-Dame de Grandchamp in Versailles, where quite late on he felt the vocation which led him to enter the diocesan major seminary in 1912. This vocation later changed direction under the influence of an older friend, the future biblical scholar Ceslas Lavergne, whose clothing as a Dominican on 7

---

17. De La Brosse, *Le Père Chenu*; Duquesne, *Un théologien en liberté*; *L'hommage différé au Père Chenu*; 'Hommage au Père M.-D. Chenu'*, in *RSPT* 75/3 (1991); *Marie-Dominique Chenu entre Moyen-Âge et modernité*; *Le Père Marie-Dominique Chenu médiéviste*, offprint of *RSPT* (1997); Florian Michel, *La pensée catholique en Amérique du Nord* (Paris: Cerf, 2010), 123–189; Étienne Fouilloux, 'Chenu' in online *Dictionnaire biographique des frères prêcheurs*.

November 1910 was attended by the young Chenu. There he was seduced by the liturgy, the community life, and the studious atmosphere of the exiled convent of the French Province, which had withdrawn to Belgium in 1903–1904. Following a year at the major seminary in Versailles, he too took the Dominican habit at Le Saulchoir, on 7 September 1913, taking the name Marie-Dominique, which definitively replaced his Christian name Marcel. Because like all religious congregations the Dominicans were forbidden from France by the secularist Republic, they attracted few vocations, and of the small number of novices fewer still persevered. His year as a recluse in the novitiate came to a brutal end, as World War 1 led to the closing of Le Saulchoir and the scattering of its religious.

Rejected for military service due to poor health on several occasions, the young Marie-Dominique was sent to Rome, where he made his simple profession on 1 December 1914, and his solemn profession an unusually long five years later. He completed his studies of philosophy and theology at the Dominican Order's Angelicum college, established as a pontifical college in 1909 [1906]. Unlike many of his contemporaries, such as Henri de Lubac who was born in 1896, entered the Jesuits in 1913, and only completed his formation in 1926, Chenu played no part at all in the conflict, which indelibly marked his contemporaries. At the Angelicum he gained a solid grounding in classical Thomist philosophy and theology, taught by professors such as Fr Hugon or Fr Lehu. Ordained priest in Rome on 19 April 1919, he completed his formation with a licentiate in theology with the university's rising star, Réginald Garrigou-Lagrange. His thesis, which he defended in 1920, dealt with the doctrine of contemplation in St Thomas Aquinas, indicating the contemplative leanings of this religious, later accounts of whose life would focus on his appetite for activity. It also marked his early refusal to dissociate thought and prayer—a refusal which would only grow stronger.[18] Although Garrigou-Lagrange wanted to make Chenu his assistant,[19] Chenu was assigned to Le Saulchoir in 1920, as was his own wish. Le Saulchoir, which his master had left for the Angelicum in 1909, had just re-opened its doors. Although he had not heard of it as a novice, he was seduced by the programme which had been drawn up in 1901 for the French Province's house of studies by its then Regent, Fr Ambroise Gardeil, for a higher school of theology which would be able to compete academically with the best universities, both public and private.[20]

2.2. Le Saulchoir

There is no better guide to Le Saulchoir than Chenu himself, in the first chapter of *Une école de théologie*, 'De Saint-Jacques au Saulchoir', which covered the history of the studies of the Friars Preachers in general, and those of the French Province in particular, from the thirteenth century onwards (pages 11–34). The final two stages merit particular attention, even though Chenu dwells on them in his own way. Let us look first at Gardeil. Fr Ambroise Gardeil, Regent of Studies from 1894 until 1911, was one of the linchpins of the reform of the programme of studies (*ratio studiorum*) imposed by the Order in 1907. In addition to the obligatory three years of philosophy and four years of theology, this programme allowed for the possibility of two further years of study specialising

---

18. Conticello, '*De contemplatione*', 363–422.
19. He requested this again, in vain, in spring 1922.
20. Camille de Belloy, 'Ambroise Gardeil: un combat pour l'étude', in *RSPT*, 92 (2008): 423–432; and Gardeil's report on studies in the French Province in 1901, 433–459.

in one of the fields of philosophy, science, or law, as well as biblical studies and history. Such access to university level study greatly enriched the Dominican formation. Gardeil himself remained a speculative thinker, but he did not discourage 'positive' thinkers; on the contrary, Fr Mannès Jacquin, who was sent to learn the discipline of history with Alfred Cauchie at the university of Louvain, later became the main architect of the *Revue des sciences philosophiques et théologiques*, founded at Le Saulchoir in 1907, the same year as the anti-Modernist encyclical *Pascendi* was published, which indicates a certain bravery.[21]

Although its Belgian exile had kept it at a distance from the Modernist storm, Le Saulchoir was not simply a spectator. Gardeil's teaching and publications, especially *Le Donné révélé et la théologie*,[22] placed him in a third group who willingly called themselves 'progressive'. Neither Modernist, nor 'anti-Modern', this third way sought to grant the legitimate demands of modernity without transgressing the limits of Catholic, Roman orthodoxy. Alongside the philosopher Maurice Blondel, the historian of early Christianity Pierre Battifol, and the Jesuit theologian Léonce de Grandmaison, we find among them, as well as Gardeil, his friend from the Toulouse Province, Marie-Joseph Lagrange, who had been responsible, with Gardeil, for the new *ratio studiorum*. The first team at Le Saulchoir felt solidarity with these mediators who suffered because of their refusal to join either side in the battle. Of course, the French Province's house of studies was hardly in the most exposed position in the fight, but its position did seem bold enough that

---

21. André Duval, 'Aux origines de la *Revue des sciences philosophiques et théologiques*', in *RSPT*, 78 (1994): 31–44.
22. (Paris: Gabalda, 1910).

a classical theologian such as Garrigou-Lagrange would feel more comfortable at the Angelicum.

Fr Antoine Lemonnyer, Regent from 1911 onwards and soon joined by Fr Pierre Mandonnet, formerly professor at Fribourg, drew together a second team at Kain once peace had returned, which the young Chenu joined. The Lemonnyer-Mandonnet stage is marked by the bursting onto the scene at Le Saulchoir of the historical method in theology. With the support of that master of medieval philosophy, Étienne Gilson, a regular at the convent for whom he provided a valued university guarantee, Le Saulchoir, under the guidance of its two leaders, committed to the huge undertaking of restoring the Angelic Doctor to his historical era. Most commentators, whose following made up the Schools, had effectively cut St Thomas off from his medieval roots and attachments, the better to contemplate his work in its logic, perfection, and permanence. The theologians at Le Saulchoir made themselves historians of the twelfth and thirteenth centuries in order to rediscover the master's sources and the initial flowering of a way of thought whose contemporaneity with the explosion of gothic architecture, the freedom of the cities, and the growth of the universities was all too often ignored: the historicity of St Thomas. To serve this, between 1921 and 1924, Le Saulchoir founded a historical institute (Institut historique d'études thomistes), the Bibliothèque thomiste series, and the Société thomiste, which published the *Bulletin thomiste*, a bibliographical supplement to the older *Revue thomiste*, founded in 1893, before winning its independence.[23] The final chapter of *Une école de*

---

23. André Duval, 'Aux origines de l'"Institut historique d'études thomistes" du Saulchoir'(1920 et ss.). Notes et documents', in *RSPT,* 75 (1991): 423–448.

théologie, 'Les études médiévales' (pages 97–105), along
with the bibliographical Appendix (pages 107–128)
proudly list the fruits of this intensive planting. 'Le
Saulchoir of Gardeil, Lemonnyer, and Mandonnet' is a
sequence which reappears frequently in Chenu's writings,
from the introduction to *Une école de théologie* until the
denouement of a crisis which he would certainly rather
have avoided, and he presented himself as the legitimate
heir to a less homogenous line than he described.

2.3. Success

Fr Chenu plunged into theological work with the
enthusiasm of youth. 'I am as happy at Le Saulchoir as
a fish in water', he wrote on 3 November 1922 to his
provincial, Fr Raymond-Marie Louis.[24] Appointed to
teach a course in the history of Christian doctrine, he was
enthusiastic about the house's Thomism, which applied
Lagrange's historical method to the Christian Middle
Ages. He undertook the secretarial work for the Institut
d'études thomistes from its founding in 1921 and in 1925
provided it with an ambitious programme; he also took
charge of the Société thomiste, writing incisive reviews in
its *Bulletin thomiste* which would win him many enemies.
His early personal works, nourished by direct contact
with the medieval sources, were erudite lexicographical
studies on words or ideas, or of the history of theology,
which took account of the cultural and social breeding
ground of the systems under discussion, in the spirit
of Lucien Febvre and Marc Bloch's *Annales d'histoire
économique et sociale*, to which he was a subscriber from
its beginnings in 1929. As professional medievalists such

---

24. Duval, 'Aux origines de l'"Institut historique d'études
thomistes" du Saulchoir', 43 n 5.

as Jacques Le Goff or Jean-Claude Schmitt have observed, he did not abandon theology for history, but his studies of the history of scholastic thought were brought to life by being situated in the context of the twelfth and thirteenth centuries.[25] This research culminated in a lengthy article published in 1927 in Étienne Gilson's journal, *Archives d'histoire doctrinale et littéraire du Moyen Âge*: 'La théologie comme science au XIIIᵉ siècle'.[26] He maintained in a classical manner that scholasticism had made theology into a true science in the Aristotelian sense of the term in the thirteenth century. But Chenu's work at Le Saulchoir went far beyond his teaching, which held a modest place in the programme of studies, and beyond his theological writing, for he showed himself to be a real organiser, soon well known for his spirit and his jokes.

This promising young theologian, then was the beneficiary of an accelerated promotion on the occasion of the Order's General Chapter which met at Le Saulchoir in July 1932, which acted as a consecration for a house whose former professor, Martin-Stanislas Gillet, had been elected Master General in 1932, having been French Provincial. It was the custom that the debates of the highest body of the Order were accompanied by an academic meeting during which one or several theologians of the host Province would take the exam known as the *ad gradus*, a staging post between the lectorate and the Master of Sacred Theology, albeit in its most basic form. Chenu was put forward, and he came through the ordeal with such panache that immediately afterwards he completed the following stage. Normally there were seven years between the *ad gradus* and the Master of Sacred Theology, but as the body of professors

---

25. *Le père Marie-Dominique Chenu médiéviste*.
26. *AHDLMA*, 2 (1927): 31–71.

did not have a Master of Sacred Theology, Gillet promoted a religious whose abilities had just been proven, to the Master of Sacred Theology without further ado. Now the most qualified of all the teaching staff, it was quite natural that Chenu should inherit the post of Regent of Studies for the start of the academic year in 1932, when he was not yet thirty-eight years of age. Who was to know at that point that a denunciation by two students had led to an initial investigation in Rome, without consequences, of the positions held at Le Saulchoir and by some of the professors there, including the new Regent?[27]

Between 1932 and 1937, Chenu's glorious Le Saulchoir went from strength to strength. Students crowded into a house which also hosted the novitiate of the Missionaries of Notre-Dame de la Salette, with no fewer than eighty entering the novitiate in the same year as Congar in 1925, including the artist, Marie-Alain Couturier, the philosopher Dominique Dubarle and the publisher Augustin-Jean Maydieu. The house of studies did not live wrapped up in its own affairs, but agreed to respond to the expectations of the chaplains and leaders of both the Belgian and then the French Jeunesse Ouvrière Chrétienne (JOC—in English known as the YCW founded by Joseph Cardijn]), who saw it as a privileged place of intellectual formation and spiritual renewal. With them it was not just the historical method, but History—with-a-capital-H—which permeated Le Saulchoir. Without abandoning

---

27. See the previous chapter. Had Chenu not been thrown by being placed on the Index and removed from Le Saulchoir, he could have found a trace of this matter in a letter of support from Canon Léon Mahieu, dean of the Faculty of Theology in Lille, dated 21 May 1942. 'I already had the opportunity some ten years ago, to say good things about the house, in response to certain attacks.'

the Middle Ages, which they had chosen, at least some of the team were invited to follow religious and secular current affairs.[28] Yet this was not enough for the Regent. 'I remained stunned and pained by the extraordinary lack of prepararedness, intellectual and moral, of so many of us Dominicans', he complained in the midst of the social crisis of spring 1936. 'It must be said that we are of our time in our philosophical and theological concerns, and information, but from the social perspective (ideas, facts, contacts), we are exiles and emigres.'[29] The decision in 1933 to acquire the property at Étiolles opened the much longed for possibility of a return to France, which would bring this exclusion to an end, although it would only become concrete five or six years later.[30]

At the invitation of Étienne Gilson, leader of a similar project in Toronto, Chenu founded the Institute of medieval studies with his Dominican confreres in Ottawa in 1930, and until 1935 he spent several months each year at this alternative Le Saulchoir, a successful spin-off across the Atlantic with which fruitful exchanges developed.[31] The *studium* of the French Province thus

---

28. M.-D. Chenu, 'La JOC au Saulchoir', in *L'Année dominicaine* (May 1936): 190–193.

29. Letter to Fr Valentin Grégoire, 14 June, ADF.

30. 'Battle is o'er! They have voted for "return"! The place chosen is Étiolles, 28 km de Paris, *20* hectares. Huge meadows (they need some fertiliser). Magnificent outbuildings, and a (very large) farm). South-facing. View over the Seine. We said a very enthusiastic Angelus with Fr Provincial *in the middle of the farm*. Deo gratias'. Card to Br Martin [Arpin], 30 October 1933, ADF.

31. Florian Michel, 'Le Saulchoir au Canada?', in *La pensée catholique en Amérique du Nord. Réseaux intellectuels et échanges culturels entre l'Europe, le Canada et les Etats-Unis (années 1920–1960)* (Paris: Desclée de Brouwer, 2010): 123–189; he was also in Ottawa when he learned he had been appointed Regent.

became a reference point for religious who lamented a formation which in their eyes was overly outmoded. In the file which holds the reactions to *Une école de théologie* there are three positive letters from Canadians, including one from the Provincial, André Bibaud,[32] and one from Noël-Marie Mailloux, 'your little brother in Canada', then studying at the Angelicum. 'Someone needed to dare to say what you have said', he wrote to Chenu on 22 January 1938. 'I don't want to judge anyone, and I do not want to forget everything I owe my masters, to whom I owe my formation, but nor do I see why I should not be allowed to show a little enthusiasm for what is going on elsewhere.' With that he ordered three copies of *Une école de théologie*, one each for himself and two of his companions. Fr Oger, assistant to the master of students of the Belgian Province, congratulated him on the ascendency of Le Saulchoir above the study houses of Belgium.[33] There are also important traces of the influence of Le Saulchoir in Britain, through the pages of *Blackfriars*, and in north Italy, in Piedmont and Lombardy. Was Le Saulchoir becoming a kind of alternative model to the Angelicum? With its combative bearing, Chenu's programmatic booklet could only reinforce such suspicions, even more so since his positions were winning hearts among the students at the Order's Roman university. Féret, briefly at the Angelicum, told Chenu, with a certain amusement, about the mockery which Garrigou-Lagrange bore the brunt of on 11 March 1937, during the speech which the Belgian religious Jacques-Marie Vosté, a former student

---

32. 'It is a door onto life in heaven and on earth', 12 February.
33. Letter dated 18 April 1938, where we also read, 'we have "discovered" someone who is your brother in spirit here, Fr Charlier'.

of the École biblique de Jérusalem and professor of Sacred Scripture, gave for the feast of St Thomas Aquinas.

He was giving a talk on the need for 'positive' work (Scripture, patristics, etc) for theology which claims to follow that of St Thomas. It was a real manifesto, developing ideas which have been undiscussed at Le Saulchoir for a long time and which the speaker [. . .] appeared to have discovered! I was dying laughing [. . .] At one point he said to the students, 'You'd be better to make the object of your thesis positive research than to lose yourself writing a thesis on Predestination!' Thunderous applause! Fr G[arrigou]-L[agrange] was red and laughing for different reasons! Realising his mistake the speaker added that of course this was not at all aimed at his friend and colleague Fr G[arrigou]-L[agrange]. More thunderous applause.[34]

Garrigou-Lagrange had collaborated on the article 'Prédestination' in the *Dictionnaire de théologie catholique* before developing his article further in a book entitled *La prédestination des saints et la grâce*.[35] Finally on 29 June 1937, came the ultimate consecration: a decree from the Congregation for Seminaries and Universities awarding pontifical status to the philosophical and theological faculties at Le Saulchoir; Fr Chenu became its first rector.[36]

Of course, Chenu was not the whole of Le Saulchoir, and he did not succeed in unifying all the lectors around a theology reinvigorated by history. Following the example

---

34. Letter dated 22 March 1937.

35. *Doctrine de saint Thomas comparée aux autres systèmes théologiques* (Bruges-Paris: Desclée de Brouwer, 1936).

36. The decree was signed by the Prefect, Cardinal Bisleti and the Secretary, Mgr Ernesto Ruffini; *Le Saulchoir Statuta Instituti philosophico-theologici Provinciae Franciae Ordinis Praedicatorum*, 52 printed pages, ADF.

of a philosopher of science, Louis-Bertrand Guérard des Lauriers, a mathematician by training, several lectors continued to hold to speculative and deductive Thomism. Some also pursued their career in a more classical setting, at the Angelicum or at Fribourg, as did the brothers Thomas and Marie-Dominique Philippe, and their namesake—no relation—Paul Philippe. Yet Chenu brought together a team who wished to renew the teaching of theology which he felt had been polluted by centuries of 'baroque' excrescences, and more recently threatened by the anti-Modernist reaction of which he had penned a veiled criticism in 1931. The philosophers Dominique Dubarle and Louis-Bertrand Geiger, and the theologians Marie-Joseph Congar and Henri-Marie Féret were the members of this troop, with whom he formed the project for a history of theology which never saw the light of day. In an early 'testimony' by Congar, unfortunately interrupted, and in a later testimony from Dubarle, we have the warm echoes of this companionship.[37] Yet the differences in methodology did not trouble the convent's studious atmosphere. 'I spent three wonderful days at Le Saulchoir', Gillet wrote to Louis, now his assistant in Rome, on 16 February 1937. 'It is a wonderful community full of drive and the Dominican spirit. St Dominic's blessing is on our Order'.[38] It was in the name of this hive of activity that on the feast of St Thomas 1936, Chenu gave the speech which was the basis for *Une école de théologie*.

---

37. Yves Congar, 'Mon témoignage', in *Journal d'un théologien, 1946–1956*, edited and introduced by Étienne Fouilloux (Paris: Cerf, 2000): 57–62; Dominique Dubarle, 'Le temps des enthousiasmes', *L'hommage différé au père Chenu*, 194–206.

38. Archives générales de l'Ordre des Prêcheurs (AGOP) V 305 (1936): 1.

2.4. An Authority

Such a burst of success granted the Regent of Le Saulchoir an authority of which he made rather pugnacious use to fight the hesitations which were starting to make themselves known in the Order about the line he was stamping on the *studium*. Garrigou-Lagrange was quite incorrect to congratulate him on his article, 'Position de la théologie',[39] which had been published in 1935, as it was almost certainly him whom Chenu had heard as a student saying that 'after all, the Incarnation is simply a *fact*; a true word spoken in jest, which openly reveals the powerlessness of speculation faced with a *fact* which gives no grasp at all to academic thought'.[40] Two especially harsh obituaries from the following year illustrate Chenu's critical verve. That of Fr Thomas Pègues, an illustrious confrere of the Toulouse Province, accused him of having raised Thomism, 'due to a lack of the necessary discernment, to an orthodoxy hardly appropriate for examining problems legitimately raised, and thus making St Thomas apparently in solidarity with the integrism of a clan where Thomism served as a cover for all sorts of dirty deeds and alliances', especially Charles Maurras' positivism. By breaking with 'these false solidarities', the Church's authority had 'granted Thomism its freedom –

---

39. 'Articles like this help me to see better the links between this new generation and the earlier one, and the *status of your work at Le Saulchoir*. Sometimes we all, and I count myself the first! – have flashes of brilliance which momentarily prevent us from understanding one another; I am pleased to be able to consider things from a better perspective through reading you', Garrigou-Lagrange wrote to Chenu having read the article; in *RSPT* 24 (1935): 232–258.

40. *RSPT*, 248.

its objectivity – against these irritating utilitarianisms'.[41] How better to suggest that that the path taken by Le Saulchoir since 1932 was the indirect consequence of the condemnation of Action française and its adherents in Catholic circles? Like the Jesuit Cardinal Louis Billot, Fr Pègues had been silenced by Pius XI's condemnation of Action française, having tried to resist. The Servite Cardinal, Alexis Lépicier, Prefect of the Congregation of Religious, was no better treated.

If being Thomist consists in accepting all of St Thomas' conclusions, from the real distinction between essence and existence to the composition of the crystalline heavens; from the physical causality of the sacraments to the theory of the four elements, Fr Lépicier was a faithful Thomist. But if the true disciple goes into the principles and mindset of his master to deal with the permanent opening and necessary progress of the fundamental problems of philosophical thought, then it must be said that Fr Lépicier [. . .] did not experience the spiritual demands of an Albert the Great or a Thomas Aquinas or, following them today, a Gardeil.[42]

Here Chenu was taking a greater risk than with Pègues, as unlike Pègues, Cardinal Lépicier had not been caught up in the resistance of those Catholics belonging to Action Française, and had died in Rome as a Cardinal with full honours.

Proof that Chenu's biting irony antagonised some of his confreres is to be found in a letter dated 29 December 1936, in which Fr Marie-Michel Labourdette, professor at the *studium* of the Toulouse Province in Saint-Maximin,

---

41. *Bulletin thomiste* (July-December 1936): 893–895 at 895; Pègues died on 28 April 1936.

42. *Bulletin thomiste*, 895 (sixteen lines all in, including the title); Lépicier died on 20 May 1936.

informed his friend Marie-Joseph Nicolas, professor at the Institut catholique de Toulouse, of plans for the *Revue thomiste* which they had just taken over. 'If the Revue thomiste has to define itself by an "anti", I wouldn't say [. . .] that it would be "anti-pragmatist", but "anti-Chenu", not personally of course, but rather his mindset and the work which to my mind is rather damaging, of this very superficial pontiff of a certain trendy Thomism.'[43] Féret's impressions from Rome are further proof, if it were needed. 'These obituaries have caused an outraged both here [generalate curia] and at the Angelicum[44] I myself have heard various echoes and complaints [. . .] I am not overly concerned, but we have enough bad press', meaning not only the obituaries, but also some of the bulletins in the *Revue des sciences*, he wrote to Chenu on 22 March 1937. He therefore counselled prudence, 'if we do not want to compromise, for a mere trifle, the task which we want to fully complete'. This was even more the case since, with the exception of Fr Simonin, former students of Le Saulchoir were hardly defending it. 'Fr Thomas Philippe, Fr Paul Philippe, and especially Fr Pollet, attached as they are to us in other areas, do not approve of us taking on this guard-dog role', he concluded. According to Fr Philipon, professor at Saint-Maximin, Garrigou-Lagrange was also considering 'a major article *against* Fr Chenu', on the latter's understanding of the relationship

---

43. Archives de la Dominican Province of Toulouse (ADT). See Michel Fourcade, 'Jacques Maritain et le renouveau de la "Revue thomiste" (1936–1940)', Serge-Thomas Bonino OP, editor, *Saint Thomas au XXᵉ siècle* (Paris: Saint-Paul, 1994), 135–152.

44. In his complaints about *Une école de théologie,* sent to Chenu in February 1938, Garrigou-Lagrange recalled Chenu's attack on Lépicier, 1.

between theological work and the spiritual life.[45] It was in fact Labourdette, as we learn from later correspondence, who had asked Garrigou-Lagrange for the article, which arrived and was sent to a reader, but never published. In the meantime its author fell out with Jacques Maritain, the mentor of the journal's new team, over the war in Spain.[46] 'Our position is too weak, especially at the point when we are going into battle against the pontiffs at Le Saulchoir, to risk falling out with Fr Garrigou. Better to ignore his ultimatiums and to stay as far away as possible from his demands', wrote Fr Bruckberger to Maritain on 14 September 1937.[47] Whatever the case, Chenu, then at Saint-Maximin, must have heard comments there about his obituary of Pègues, which had caused great displeasure.[48] So even before *Une école de théologie* was published, the hostile reactions from the Angelicum and Saint-Maximin were foreseeable, so clear-cut seemed the divisions between the two camps of Thomism.

Chenu did not limit himself to intervening in theological questions. He was passionate about the work of his confreres at the Éditions du Cerf, where Gillet had refused to assign him so as not to destabilise

---

45. Letter from Labourdette to Nicolas, dated 1 June 1937, ADT.

46. Of course Garrigou-Lagrange discussed Chenu's statement that the division between the ascetic and the mystic was 'infuriating' in a review of Mandonnet's *Notre vie divine* (*Bulletin thomiste*, July-December 1936: 784–789), in 'L'axe de la vie spirituelle et son unité' (*Revue thomiste* 43 (1937): 347–360), but this brief discussion is hardly the heralded 'major article'.

47. Letter quoted in Fourcade, 151.

48. Letter from Labourdette to Nicolas, 9 June 1937, ADT. Nonetheless *Revue thomiste* would publish his article, 'Le plan de la Somme théologique de saint Thomas', *Revue thomiste*, 45 (1939): 93–107.

Le Saulchoir,[49] and he made use of his new authority to defend them against political attacks, which increased from 1936 onwards. He was therefore far from unknown in Rome when *Une école de théologie* was published. As we read in the draft of a letter sent on 31 August 1937 to Louis, 'I might add that from now on rather leaving these calumnies be [. . .], I shall sometimes make myself respond despite my disgust.' We find a series of these interventions among his papers. Paul Vignaux, a disciple of Gilson as a medieval philosopher and the founder of the Syndicat Général de l'Éducation Nationale [General National Education Union], was therefore correct to relocate the Chenu affair within the context of 'his political connections, from the war in Ethiopia to the Vichy regime'.[50] Following Pius XI's condemnation of Action Française, Marie-Vincent Bernadot and his assistants had founded in quick succession *La Vie intellectuelle* (1928), the Éditions du Cerf (1929), and the weekly *Sept* (1934) to maintain and support the papal line.[51] This flank of the French Cactholic Church had the wind in its sails as long as it had the support of the pope; but the wind in Rome changed following the Italian attack on Ethiopia, when *Sept*'s reservations on the matter caused a reaction in fascist circles and within Italian Catholicism. Guido Manacorda, until now a friend of the Order, who held the chair of comparative literature in Florence, and a fascist who had recently converted to Catholicism, began to specialise in denouncing the supposed links between the

---

49. Letter to Fr Marie-Vincent Bernadot, who thanked him for it, 6 April 1931, Archives des Éditions du Cerf.
50. Introduction to the 1987 re-edition in his *Philosophie au Moyen Âge* (Paris: Vrin, 2004), 50, n 1.
51. Étienne Fouilloux, *Les Éditions dominicaines du Cerf, 1918-1965* (Rennes: Presses universitaires de Rennes, 2018).

French Dominicans and freemasonry or communism. 'We are astounded by the improbable calumnies which men of the stature of Professor Manacorda himself publish. We wonder whether they 'read' those whom they criticise in this way. These calumnies are of the same level of those in the German papers at the moment about parish and clergy conspiring with communism', Chenu wrote to a confrere in Milan, Fr Enrico Brianza, who ensured a clarification was received.[52] The attacks increased as the Popular Front came to power in France and the outbreak of the civil war in Spain. *Sept*'s refusal to align with either side, like that of Maritain, quickly became untenable. Wrongly accused of 'red Christian' sympathies, *Sept* was suppressed by a decree of the Holy Office on 14 July 1937, its final issue appearing on 27 August.[53] Chenu protested strongly to Gillet and Louis about this measure, even though he had 'no doctrinal responsibility' for the journal. 'I cannot hide from you that for the young generation of your sons, as for a whole generation of apostles in France, this is a defeat which in truth and charity, depresses us', he wrote to the Master General.[54]

At the start of September 1937, he contacted the influential Jesuit, Enrico Rosa, editor of the *Civiltà cattolica* since 1931, to contest certain references in

---

52. Passage quoted in French in Brianza's reply to the editor of the Ferrara *Corriere padano*, 18 July 1937, copy attached to his letter to Chenu dated 20 juillet.

53. Martine Sévegrand, *Temps Présent. Une aventure chrétienne*. Volume 1: l'hebdomadaire, 1937–1947 (Paris: Éditions du Temps Présent, 2006), 17–28; Magali Della Sudda, 'Le Vatican, la France et l'hebdomadaire *Sept*' in *Vingtième siècle. Revue d'histoire* (October-December 2009): 29–44.

54. Undated draft of letter; and draft of letter to Fr Louis, 31 August.

his recent article, 'Catholicisme et maçonnerie', which lent credence to the rumours of collusion between the French Dominicans and the 'masons'. Subtitled 'L'appel d'un maçon à la trêve',[55] the article referred to Albert Lantoine's *Lettre au Souverain Pontife* which Manacorda and *La France réelle*, a mouthpiece of the extreme right, had already picked up on. Chenu only received a polite response.[56] At the same time he sent a note to several members of the French hierarchy, in which he denounced Manacorda's campaign and appeal to Rome against the Dominicans. 'If Sept must die today, it is almost certainly for economic reasons' – the reason Gillet had given to protect the apostolic secret—'but it is also because of pressure from similar campaigns of calumny, in Italy and in France which, despite their crassness, are not entirely ineffective', he wrote, rather perceptively.[57] The replies which he received shake up received ideas about the French episcopate. While Cardinal Liénart of Lille was easily convinced,[58] it was Mgr Feltin, archbishop of Bordeaux, who most shared the theologian's perspective, judging the end of *Sept* to be 'most regrettable', while Cardinal Suhard, archbishop of Rouen, contented himself with an emollient note of acknowledgement.[59]

---

55. *La Civiltà Cattolica* (10 August 1937): 289–301.

56. Draft of letter dated 1 September and reply dated 25 September.

57. Draft among his papers along with another which feared that 'the Order's official silence will, through the clear contrast, give rise to public wickedness'.

58. Letter date 11 September and confirmed on 15 September by Fr Thomas Delos, professor at the Catholic university of Lille.

59. Replies dated 10 and 20 September (Chenu noted '*satis episcopaliter*' in the margins).

Next Chenu contacted Louis on 8 October, to warn him about a condemnation of *La Vie intellectuelle*, which also felt under threat. 'As *Sept* has gone, now it is *La Vie intellectuelle* which is subject to attack', in which he saw a major offensive against the forces of progress within French Catholicism: 'attacks against VI, an (aborted) attempt to reintroduce A. F. into the Church, corrections in the JOC against Cardijn's inspiration, discreet threats of a growing integrism in the fields of exegesis, history, and philosophy'.[60] This correspondence was poorly timed, as Gillet had just removed Chenu as censor of the review, which had devolved to Le Saulchoir, while Louis was complaining about too many high-risk articles, whether on Rousseau or Rimbaud,[61] just as the Guillemin matter— of which Chenu, naturally, knew nothing—was brewing.[62] 'Christianus is *excellent*, and his balanced thought allows him to be so bold. Go ahead. Are you putting Guillemin's "*Par notre faute*" in the same issue of V. I., as it is in the proofs? That article is just in time to illustrate E. Borne's note. *Nihil obstat*, for the whole issue', he had written to Fr Maydieu, the editor, before being removed as censor.[63] '*L'Église corps de péché*', *Christianus*' note, penned by the philosopher Étienne Borne, and the article by the literature scholar Henri Guillemin, 'Par notre faute', went to press on 10 September 1937. Their title described the content in glorious technicolour: the repeated faults of

---

60. Draft of the letter.

61. Letter dated 11 October.

62. Draft of a letter to Louis dated 23 October. He could not stop himself noting 'derision of circumstances that Le Saulchoir can have a university shop window, administrative confidence faced with lack of doctrinal trust' (the *studium* had just been granted the canonical status of a pontifical university for its philosophy and theological faculties).

63. Undated letter, Archives des Éditions du Cerf.

the church down the centuries and still today, were partly responsible for the loss of so many of her children.[64] It is an understatement to say that Guillemin's article made a poor impression. 'Here it has scandalised many', wrote Gillet, astounded at its publication, from Indochina.[65]

It was therefore fortunate that *La Vie intellectuelle* escaped with only a warning from the official tasked with this work, the Italian Dominican Mariano Cordovani, Master of the Apostolic Palace. In *L'Osservatore Romano* of Sunday 14 November, he put his name to a front-page article, entitled, *'Per un articolo stampato nella Rivista "La Vie Intellectuelle"'*, a severe criticism of Guillemin's article which ended with *'le Censeur aurait dû censurer'* in italics. Rather than keeping quiet, Chenu, whose concern for honesty verged on naivety, made amends to the Italian religious who had taught him at the Angelicum.[66] Much to the annoyance of Louis,[67] he brought himself to the attention of this influential person who until then had not known the identity of the censor. Cordovani replied cordially, but without giving an inch on the need for his authorised warning.[68] We shall soon see him lining up against *Une école de théologie*. 'Several of our readers have made us aware of the painful astonishment they

---

64. Michel Fourcade, 'L'affaire *"Par notre faute"'*, in *Mélanges offerts à Gérard Cholvy* (Montpellier, 2003): 151–168.

65. Letter to his assistant, Louis, AGOP V 305 1936 (1).

66. Draft of a letter dated 16 November.

67. 'If he [Louis] had received the original he would have hesitated to send it on before having been in touch with you, wrongly convinced as he is that no one here, apart from himself and Cordovani, knew until this morning's post who the censor responsible for this was', he wrote to Chenu having received a copy of the letter to Cordovani, card dated 19 November.

68. Letter dated 19 November.

were caused by two articles which appeared in the issue dated 10 September. We have asked their forgiveness', acknowledged the issue of 10 November. 'The following pages will prove to them that *La Vie Intellectuelle* remains worthy of their confidence and their esteem, and that it has truly inherited our elders' filial piety for God's holy Church.' There followed a note by Christianus, entitled '*Sainte Église*', and on the letters page a translation of Cordovani's article with an introductory paragraph in which the editorial team acknowledged that 'we were wrong to publish these two articles'. *La Vie intellectuelle* carried on, but the guillotine had come very close: it had just escaped being suppressed only weeks after *Sept*.

This flood of adventures confirms that the decade of idyllic relations between Rome and the fighting flank of French Catholicism, following Pius XI's condemnation of Action Française, had truly come to an end by 1937. The days of the Popular Front drew the pendulum of Vatican fears towards the left. In these damaged circumstances the Regent of Le Saulchoir had indicated to the superiors of the Order and to certain circles in the curia that he was one of the main theological guarantees of the publications of his confreres at Éditions du Cerf, which was increasingly threatened. The difficulties of *Une école de théologie* have probably been overly removed from this environment. Chenu's positions on theological method would be examined with a much more pernickety eye because, in the eyes of both his superiors and the Roman Province, he had more or less become the spokesman for the audacity of the French Province.

3. A Favourable Reception

Une école de théologie, a booklet with a tiny print run, not distributed in the usual commercial way, and soon withdrawn from sale, had a limited distribution, as proven by the almost total absence of reviews. How then can we imagine its reception? The house chronicle at Le Saulchoir emphasises that Chenu 'continually receives enthusiastic approval and congratulations from the most varied and authoritative theological and Thomist circles and people (Paris, Louvain, Strasbourg, Saint-Alban, Oxford, etc.)'[69] He kept this armful of responses, in which regret at its withdrawal soon overpowered acknowledgements of receipt. Thirty-one reactions have come to us in this way, twenty-one from Dominican confreres and ten from those outside of the Order. His old friend Mgr Roger Beaussart, Auxiliary Bishop of Paris, to whom the booklet was dedicated and who did not understand the 'misinterpretations' of Chenu's thought;[70] Mgr Bruno de Solages, Rector of the Institut catholique de Toulouse; Fr Émile Amann, professor at the theology faculty at Strasbourg and editor of the *Dictionnaire de théologie catholique*; Fr Lucien Cerfaux, an exegetical scholar at Louvain and friend of Le Saulchoir;[71] Fr Charles Journet, professor at the major seminary in Fribourg in Switzerland; the Jesuits Ferdinand Cavallera, from the Institut catholique de Toulouse, Henri de Lubac, at the Catholic faculty in Lyon, and Blaise Romeyer, at the scholasticate in Vals-près-Le Puy; and finally the lay university professors Aimé Forest and Étienne Gilson, who defended Chenu to Gillet.[72]

---

69. 31 January, ADF.

70. Letters dated 21 and 28 February 1938.

71. 'Your booklet makes me think that I have developed under the profound influence of the mind-set of Fr Lemonnyer, whom I continue to truly worship', he wrote to Chenu on 14 January 1938.

72. Letter to Chenu dated 29 March 1938, FA Murphy, 'Correspondance entre É. Gilson et M.-D. Chenu: un choix de lettres, 1923-1969'. In *Revue thomiste*: 105 (2005): 41–43.

Twenty-seven of these reactions were favourable, even enthusiastic, including that of Sertillanges, who had returned to Le Saulchoir having been under a shadow for a long time and knew what it was to be under suspicion.[73] We should also note the difference in support which came from the other two French houses of study. The only favourable sound from Saint-Maximin came from Philippon, and must be weighed against the clear support from Saint-Alban-Leysse, the *studium* of the Lyon Province, penned by Frs Bouëssé and Gerlaud. Note, too, the significance of support from different spiritual families: the Jesuits Henri de Lubac, without any reservations,[74] and Ferdinand Cavallera, with some reservations, or the convinced Thomist Aimé Forest who did not spare his admiration.[75] Finally, and not insignificantly, as they were Dominicans, we must note that several of those who wrote to the author – Charlier, Delos, Lagrange, and Simonin – were quick to describe *Une école de théologie* as a 'manifesto': far from seeing their use of the word as some kind of verbal inflation, they testify that Chenu's work was certainly considered by several of his defenders to be a manifesto. Some of his closest friends expressed some reservations about the pugnacious nature of many of his phrases: this was certainly the case for Féret, although we have no trace of

---

73. Letter to Fr Antonin Motte, Prior of Le Saulchoir, ADF.

74. 'May the school of Le Saulchoir contribute more and more to the realisation of the *presence* of a truly *Catholic* theology in our times!', Letter dated 18 March 1938.

75. Card dated 24 January 1938.

his opinion,[76] and more explicitly for Congar. 'It is not about whether I would have written everything which you have written, and whether I would have written it in that way. Of course, some passages of the book are lacking in a certain calmness, and there are some points which I would have put in another way', he confided to Chenu on 1 February 1938 in a letter of warmth and solidarity, in which he pleaded with him not to let Rome impose anything on him, 'at the cost of our dishonour'.[77]

Only four reactions contrast with this chorus of praise, and then regrets: three deplore Chenu's audacity, and one alone judges it insufficient. This was the opinion of Fr Henri-Dominique Simonin, a former pupil at Le Saulchoir, now at the Angelicum, whose differences with Chenu went back some time but had no public expression. 'Fr Simonin, who criticises us sharply when he writes to us, never says anything against us when he is with his colleagues, and rather represents our spirit rather well there, whether he wishes to or not. I even think that his severity when he writes to us partly stems from the fact that he sees very well that we are rather too happy to play with fire here, and risk receiving a harsh blow which will compromise the serious work which we wish to serve and which he like us also wishes to serve', Féret observed to Chenu.[78] 'I am not in agreement with either the content or the form', Simonin wrote to Chenu. The charge was brusque, Simonin writing:

---

76. 'On the matter of Fr Chenu, what you have said is quite right. He is paved with good intentions (rather like the road to hell)', Fr Simonin wrote to him on 6 November 1938, Féret papers, ADF.

77. Letter of acknowledgement to Chenu, Rome, 3 February, Congar papers, ADF.

78. Letter from Rome, 22 March 1937.

> As to its form, the work is unacceptable both from
> an administrative perspective (this is not the style
> of a rector of ecclesiastical faculties) and from a
> technical perspective, as it is not the theological
> style in which one can clearly propose an attempt at
> methodology. As for the content, once we scratch
> off the surface and abstract from the particular
> style of presentation, we only find the Gardeil-
> Garrigou position [. . .] which I myself can no
> longer tolerate [. . .] Why surround a backwards,
> outdated position with dubious formulas. What is
> the point?

On the other hand, he noted substantial agreement with
Charlier's *Essai sur le problème théologique* to the extent
that it removed theology from its speculative mould to
place it at the service of the life of the Church.[79] One of
the rare criticisms of *Une école de théologie*, outside of
the Roman trial, which has come down to us, complains
that it does not go far enough in rejecting its scholastic
heritage.

On the other hand, three confreres complained of
Chenu's excessive audacity. Labourdette's opinion that
'even Fr Lagrange himself is unhappy with Chenu's
booklet', and 'would have made himself heard to the
author in his reply',[80] is surprising given the letter from
the former exegete, now retired to Saint-Maximin. He
welcomed the 'wonderful things' Chenu had written
about the École biblique and in particular 'this organically
revived theology' whose programme he himself had
drawn up. Neither did he contest the genealogy of Le

---

79. Letter dated 6 November 1938; Simonin's reservation were
    reported to the Regent of Le Saulchoir in a meeting in Rome
    at the start of February, letter to Chenu, 20 February.
80. Letter to Nicolas, 21-22 January 1938, ADT.

Saulchoir. As for Gardeil, while he had had 'sparks of light, it was impossible for me to recognise an overarching unity or synthesis in his work. He would have had difficulty admitting that a Dominican should not dedicate himself wholly to the thought of St Thomas.' And Mandonnet? 'I must say I have always regarded him as mediocre', admitted Lagrange, without embarrassing himself with nuances. 'It goes without saying that your own work has grown and magnified it', he added, crediting Chenu alone with the renown of the house, having destroyed its foundations. 'Another story of hum-drum traditionalists', he wrote to his disciple in Jerusalem, Roland de Vaux, about the Chenu affair, in one of his final letters, since he died on 10 March 1938.[81].

Labourdette was harsh in other ways in his correspondence with Nicolas. 'Fr Chenu has just published a manifesto [. . .] It is a statement of principles, not lacking the inherent naivety of the genre, increased by the satisfaction which a rather narrow circle has of [?].' So much for the form. On the content, alongside 'many common ideas', Labourdette complained about finding 'that equivocal idea of religious experience'. In this Chenu was returning to Molinism and, what was worse, 'to the worst of Blondel, the one who wanted to transform Thomas' definition of the truth into "adaequatio mentis et vitae"', the ancient complaint of Garrigou-Lagrange to Blondel. The two main errors of *Une école de théologie* on religious experience and the nature of understanding would make 'advances' to Maritain 'from head to toe'. Yet this was not the opinion of Charles Journet, Maritain's theologian reference point. The booklet, of which he requested a copy from Chenu since he was unable to procure one himself, seemed to him to be 'certainly

---

81. Letters dated 8 January and 9 February, ADT.

directed against Fr Garrigou-Lagrange ', 'or rather against
what is sclerotic and authoritarian in his contemporary
writings [. . .] But as a whole (aside from a certain
philosophical agnosticism) it seems to me to be a very clear
homage to *Degrés du savoir*', he wrote to Maritain on 23
April 1938.[82] Thomas Philippe's embarrassment was very
obvious–he who had left Le Saulchoir for the Angelicum
in 1936. In his card of 17 January 1938 he covertly
expressed his reservations about the links established by
Chenu between contemplation and theology as a science:
of course 'contemplation is useful and even necessary for
theology to flourish, but is this necessity attached to the
very structure of theological science?' Philippe did not
respond, but we can sense where his preference would
lie. His reservations, and Labourette's even more so, lay
promise to a difficult future.

4. Rome, 1938

'How will your booklet be received there?', wrote Humbert
Bouëssé to Chenu.[83] 'Those poor French Dominicans will
definitely look like revolutionaries. Clearly the life and
work at Le Saulchoir are somewhat humiliating for the
international university.' He did not know how true his
words were. On 3 January 1938, Louis, heading the Order
on behalf of Gillet, who was then undertaking a series
of visitations to Dominican foundations in Indochina,
congratulated him on the reception of *Une école de
théologie*. 'Interested in, and even very enthusiastic
about' the work, he asked Chenu, with the agreement of
Fr Michael Browne, Rector of the Angelicum, to send a

---

82. Journet-Maritain *Correspondance*, volume II, 1930–1939
    (Fribourg/Paris, 1997), 728–729.
83. Letter dated 25 January.

further copy for Mgr Ernesto Ruffini, Secretary to the Congregation for seminaries and universities.[84] But on 14 January, the instruction was rescinded, as two religious who knew Ruffini well 'reckon that some of the ideas which you express in the work are not likely to please him, and it's better not to present him with it'. This was a busy time for the Holy Office in censoring books, and Ruffini was a well-known heresy hunter. On 17 January, Fr Jourdain Padé, the French Provincial travelling to Rome, confirmed that Browne had stated that 'we must not allow Fr Chenu's ideas to be passed on'; and another religious who was consulted said that 'while there has been no formal protest against your way of thinking and writing, the Angelicum had no reason for this. The Holy Office must not be informed, otherwise things will get nasty'. Padé also sent a telegram to stop sales of the booklet until he had more information. 'In the aftermath of the Latour-Maubourg affair this setback is considered most untoward here. I see plenty of people who are very wound up', he wrote. Labourdette confirmed to his friend Nicolas that 'Fr Chenu's stupid booklet is stirring up the Anglicum, Fr Garrigou has written an awful letter about it. If it were only him it wouldn't be so surprising and there wouldn't be so much to fear, but it is Fr Browne . . . who has raised the alarm and is expressing his outrage. Fr Garrigou is hoping that since the booklet isn't for sale it will not reach the Congregation for Studies, since it contains sharp criticisms of the *rationes studiorum*, including the one currently in force.' According to Garrigou, 'the author gives the impression of a bus driver who is going far too fast on a road where there are very dangerous turns'.[85] In this way the affair took on the

---

84. Letters dated 3 and 11 January 1948.
85. Undated letter, ADT.

aspect of a settling of accounts between the Angelicum and Le Saulchoir. The dispute was nothing new: we might think it even preceded Chenu's preference for Kain in 1920 against Garrigou-Lagrange's advice,[86] but his regency had hardly calmed matters. 'Only our Fathers at the Angelicum—at least some of them, who are also the most influential there—saw the positions which are dangerous for the faith, and in particular for the position of theology' in *Une école de théologie*, was the summary of the house chronicle of Le Saulchoir, in support of Chenu.

Fr Garrigou-Lagrange, then vice-rector of the Angelicum, expressed his grievances in a hand-written note, probably given to Chenu during their meeting in Rome, which Chenu commented on in the margins.[87] Having praised the 'elevated conception of the supernaturality of faith' contained in *Une école de théologie*, alongside its appeal to 'the interior life', and even 'the contemplative life for the Thomist theologian', he first of all regretted its style. Chenu seemed to be 'too sure of himself: and sometimes a bitterness which has allowed it to be said that the tone is sometimes hateful, the tone of a speech for the defence which is often unjust to others', much stronger in any case than Gardeil and Lemonnyer, whom Chenu incorrectly claimed to follow. Garrigou-Lagrange wondered whether the booklet would not 'do more harm than good', among the young students and even the young professors whose philosophical incompetence was noted during the *ad gradus* exam,

---

86. 'Allow me to remind you that ni 1919, after World War 1, Fr G[arrigou]-L[agrange] tried to prevent the *Revue* [*des sciences philosophiques et théologiques*, Le Saulchoir's 'house journal'] from starting up again', draft of a letter from Chenu to the Provincial, Antonin, undated (May 1943).

87. 'Une école de théologie', undated, 5pp.

the Roman stage before the Master of Sacred Theology. Among other exaggerated criticisms, he focused on those against the *ratio studiorum*, against the Thomist manuals for philosophy and theology, and against the 'great Thomists of the 16th and 17th centuries', whom Chenu said were over obsessed with the fight against Protestantism. As an author of manuals and a disciple of the commentators on St Thomas Aquinas, Garrigou-Lagrange could not but see himself as the target of these criticisms, which are everywhere in *Une école de théologie*. Several of his reservations on the content would live long: understatement of the Modernist crisis, confusion between 'theology and the theologian's religious experience', relativisation of dogmatic statements through the history of metaphysics. En route Garrigou-Lagrange picked up on the shock-formulas which numerous censors would also note: 'There was no greater disgrace for Thomism than to be treated as an orthodoxy', without the inverted commas around orthodoxy which changed the word's meaning. 'It was also a great honour for St Thomas to see that his formulas served the Council of Trent and the (First) Vatican Council', he retorted.

Forewarned about the 'tendentious interpretation' and 'misinterpretations given to [his] work', Chenu sought a face-to-face meeting with Browne to dispel them. *Une école de théologie* simply developed his article, 'Position de la théologie', which at the time of publication had been praised by Garrigou-Lagrange.[88] Browne accepted all this, while indicating that 'several phrases' in the publication 'would require an explanation'. 'I saw Fr Browne at length', Padé confirmed. 'Pained and anxious', he 'had made a note of 55 passages which were more or less illicit' in his

88. Draft of undated letter, and reply dated 21 January.

copy, which the Provincial sent to Le Saulchoir.[89] 'I have studied the system of pen strokes closely', Chenu wrote to Dubarle, 'and I must say that I was struck by the array. Let us put some points to one side, along with the attacks on the spirit of constructing a mental construct; against reducing thought to systems. There are two points at stake. A. The mind-set and economy of intellectual research. B. The very status of "sacred doctrine". The second point seems more serious to him: 'it is the key understanding of the concept of the status of theology which are at stake with these coachmen.' To Dubarle's eye, there was more than one misunderstanding between Chenu and his Roman critics based on misinterpretations: a really basic divergence on the nature and function of theology.[90]

'I saw Fr Garrigou, strident yet fraternal', Padé added on 17 January. 'He makes the same complaints as Fr Browne, although he adds some regrets about the severity of your judgements on the old scholastics and the manuals.' And he repented of his letter praising the article 'Position de la théologie', which risked opposing him to Chenu.[91] The provincial had also recently met Cordovani, who had the booklet in his hands and had annotated

---

89. Letter dated 27 January, which arrived 30 January, although this is not the one which Fr André Duval kept, on which he clarified, 'the red marks in the margin or in the text correspond to the passages underlined by Fr Garrigou-Lagrange in his personal copy. Unfortunately I did not note the series of indiscretions which meant this information came to me.'

90. Letter sent to Rome, 1 February.

91. Letter quoted. On 2 February, Dubarle completed his analysis of Browne's pen marks with a 'parallel between a certain number of texts in your booklet challenged by ticks and texts from Garrigou's *De Revelatione* (see too the letter from Hyacinthe Dondaine dated 3 February).

thirty-one of the most contested passages.[92] According to Cordovani, Master of the Apostolic Palace, 'the work as it is presented, by the Rector of a faculty [of theology], cannot be defended, even by Fr Chenu's best friend. It stinks of Modernism and subjectivism.' Nothing less. If it came to the attention of Ruffini or the Holy Office, it was at risk of being condemned, for Thomism came out of it as 'disqualified'. Cordovani knew what he was talking about, as he himself had just called *La Vie intellectuelle* and its censor, one Marie-Dominique Chenu, to order. On 28 January, Louis invited Chenu, now incessantly howling about the trial of the intention and seeking mediation with the absent Master General, to come to explain himself to his opponents.[93] Having left Le Saulchoir on 31 January, he arrived in Rome in the evening of 1 February.

The letter which Louis sent to Padé on Sunday 6 February gives a glimpse of the Roman visit. 'As you know, Fr Chenu arrived here on Tuesday evening . . . from the very next morning, he began paying visits, and everywhere received a very charitable welcome. While no one shared his opinion, it seemed to him that he found much understanding from some.' Chenu would therefore have carried out a series of personal visits, without appearing before a commission. 'On Thursday evening, he had seen all those he had to see', continued Louis, 'and so I arranged a meeting the next day with Fr Regent to know what else was to be done, since Fr Chenu had withdrawn his book from publication and agreed to write an article, in which he would clearly set out his thought and which

---

92. Emilio Panella notes them on Cordovani's copy, 'Due maestri in una scuola di teologia', pages 169–176; see too the earlier Raimondo Spiazzi, *P. Mariano Cordovani dei Frati predicatori* (Rome: 1954).

93. Draft of a letter, undated, and Louis' reply dated 28 February.

would be submitted to the censors before publication. Before I could explain my thoughts, Fr Regent stated that he had just seen Fr Cordovani, who was still convinced that if the book was denounced it would be condemned, and that we should think about taking the precaution of making Fr Chenu sign propositions, giving me the text.' This list had been drawn up by a commission of three members, 'not well balanced', according to Simonin, since the only Frenchman, Garrigou-Lagrange, 'was judge and jury in the whole affair, and the other two had been chosen from among those who would be the least able to really understand your writings'.[94] Louis continued, 'Having read them, I asked [Fr Regent] if we really needed to do this. As he insisted, I told him I would take them to Fr Chenu, who did not resist signing them. I shall not say he has done so, and I ask you not to do so either. It is simply a document I shall keep to one side in case we are asked for explanations, which I hope will not happen.' Was Chenu also asked to publish a commentary on these propositions, as Garrigou-Langrange claimed in 1942?[95] Whatever the case, he did not.

---

94. Letter to Chenu dated 20 February. These others are the Belgian Mannès Matthijs, dean of the theology faculty at the Angelicum, who thought it was not politic to meet Chenu, and the German Anselme Rohner who taught there (his name only appears in the documents collected by Fr Garrigou-Lagrange for his visitation of Le Saulchoir in 1942; among those who examined the booklet he lists Cordovani, Browne, himself, Matthijs and Rohner; typed pages in his archives from Fr Paul Coutagne).

95. 'Insuper P. Browne ut Rector Coll. Ang. in nomini Vicarii dixit ad P. Chenu ut suscriberet quibusdam propo. circa nat. theol. et evolutio. dogm., et ut scriberet suo modo circa has propositiones. P. Chenu hoc non fecit' (same source).

The ten propositions produced by Cordovani, perhaps drawn up by Browne, were published in facsimile in the re-edition of *Une école de théologie* in 1985.[96] The first agrees that 'dogmatic formulas express an absolute and unchanging truth', the second that 'in philosophy as in theology, true and certain propositions are firm and not fragile in any way'. The third states that Revelation ended with the death of the last apostle and that Tradition does not create new truths, and the fourth that theology is not a spirituality which has found tools suitable for its religious experience, but a true science ordered to the faith. The fifth affirms that the different theological systems are not equally true with regard to the subjects in which they diverge, and the sixth that St Thomas' system is truly orthodox, in other words, that it conforms to the truths of faith. The seventh says that according to St Thomas, it is necessary to demonstrate theological truths by Scripture and Tradition, not only through reason, and the eighth that St Thomas, authentically a theologian, was also authentically a philosopher, and that, consequently, the intelligibility and truth of his philosophy are not dependent on his theology. The ninth states that, in his academic work, the theologian must stick to Thomas' metaphysics and the rules of dialectic, and the tenth that other authors and teachers must be respected in speech and in writing, even while indicating their errors.

Were the story not so serious, such a list would raise a smile. Chenu had much less difficulty signing it, since he felt that he had never expressed any proposition which opposed this list. Thus, he was obliged to agree to the orthodoxy of Thomism, without inverted commas, while he had written that Thomism had been treated as though it were an 'orthodoxy' with inverted commas, in other

---

96. To be found on page 35.

words as a closed system impervious to any adaptations. Chenu however was wrong not to see the clumsy or even malevolent caricature of his position in this syllabus. The text submitted to him simply listed the criticisms made of his booklet, to which it referred in no uncertain terms: Chenu had indeed written that 'a theology worthy of the name is a spirituality which has found the rational tools which serve its religious experience'. The difference between him and his confreres at the Angelicum was therefore not simply mud-slinging, but a fundamental disagreement about what theology is and should be: the rigid, abstract conception contained in the formulas which he had to sign is the polar opposite of the historical and spiritual understanding illustrated by his booklet, in which his censors rightly saw a quite radical questioning of their vision of Thomism and an alternative model which could replace it.

Born of the sharp reaction at the Angelicum to *Une école de théologie*, the matter was restricted to the Roman tribunal of the Dominican Order. Of course 'the Master of the Sacred Palace is the Vatican';[97] and Fr Emilio Panella has clearly shown how hostile Cordovani was to Chenu's ideas, having recently reprimanded him over *La Vie Intellectuelle*. But nothing of this hostility showed through for now. In Rome, Chenu had been able to count on the support of Louis and some others from Le Saulchoir, where those faithful to him formed a block around him. With Congar, Féret, Geiger, and particularly Dubarle, he had a real 'brain trust' who worked to defend him, and the *studium* as a whole. Nonetheless he returned to Le Saulchoir 'rather battered', for his ideas had clashed with the 'discouraging incomprehension' which proved the reality of the 'ruptures and dissociations in some

---

97. Letter from Labourdette to Nicolas, 5 February 1938, ADT.

post-Tridentine theology' denounced by his booklet.[98] However the fever seemed to break after his return. He heard from Rome that his accusers were 'fighting a rearguard action': their complaints against his booklet had been 'more opportunistic than doctrinal'.[99] Louis now hoped that there would be no 'new troubles' arising, after months of difficulties for the French Province: the suppression *Sept* in August 1937, threats against *la vie intellectuelle* in November 1937 and Le Saulchoir in February 1938. This really was too much.[100]

Chenu's authority was not diminished by the crisis. On 30 May 1938 a letter from Gillet, now returned from Indochina, ordered him to write 'a short but substantial little report on the importance of the science of history in our days and in our Order', in order to convince the next General Chapter. This order is surprising, for the overimportance granted to history in the formation of future theologians was precisely one of the points of friction between Chenu and his censors. Chenu carried out the task with the enthusiasm we might expect, but it was Oxford, not Le Saulchoir, which was to found a specialist institute, as the French Province's *studium* was to be the home of an institute for social sciences.[101] Chenu did however play an important role in the General Chapter which was held in the new home of the General Curia at Santa Sabina from 25 to 28 September 1938, as a member of the commission for studies, where he met Fr Matthijs again, a member of the commission for the tertiaries, and

---

98. Le Saulchoir house chronicle, 11 February, ADF.

99. Letters from Fr Mathiot, 11 March and 13 April.

100. Lettre quoted to Padé dated 6 February.

101. *Acta capituli generalis*, vote, pages 38–39; and note '*De studiis historicis*', signed by Gillet, pages 44–51.

the president of the commission for economic affairs.[102] He was also the linchpin of the founding of a working group on Islam, announced to the Chapter fathers *sub secreto* by Gillet, a team which would become the Institut dominicain d'études orientales in Cairo.[103] And Chenu too presided over the return of the *studium* to France, for which the Province had been preparing for years. 'In October at least a group needs to occupy the house at Étiolles, symbolically and in fact', Dubarle wrote to him on 7 February. It was accomplished for the start of the university academic year in 1938, with the philosophy students living in the great house, near Corbeil, before the theologians, who arrived just war broke out.[104]

5. More Storm Clouds

The calm before the storm was short. A few months later in 1937, it was Congar's *Chrétiens désunis* which was threatened with censure. This great book by the thirty-three-year-old theologian, which opened the way to a 'Catholic "ecumenism"', was the first volume in the '*Unam Sanctam*' series, a collection of ecclesiological and ecumenical studies, whose series editor at the Éditions du Cerf was Congar himself. Chenu welcomed its publication enthusiastically, seeing in it 'one of the most beautiful fruits of our theology here at Le Saulchoir, where the return to the sources and the principles, the historical

---

102. *Acta capituli generalis,* pages 23, 25 and 26.

103. Dominique Avon, *Les Frères prêcheurs en Orient. Les dominicains du Caire (années 1920-années 1960)* (Paris: Cerf, 2005), 337-42.

104. 'Our removals arrived by barge on 2 September 1939', Yves Congar, *Une vie pour la vérité, Jean Puyo interroge le Père Congar* (Paris: Le Centurion, 1975), 85.

realism of the Incarnation, the light of the contemplation of faith, give a youthful and triumphant seduction to the traditional "conclusions'".[105] Having labelled Le Saulchoir in this way, this pioneering work was given as favourable a welcome in Catholic circles as by the 'separated brethren', whether Orthodox, Anglican, or Reformed, which might make more hardline readers frown.[106]

5.1. Congar's Ecumenism

There were very few discordant voices in the concerto of praise. British Catholic newspapers, such as the *Catholic Herald*, of course regretted a certain *irenism*, which risked putting the brakes on the increase in conversions,[107] but more nuanced reviews focused less on the ecumenism in *Chrétiens désunis* than the methodology of which it was the fruit. Several kindly readers noted in passing Congar's excessive indulgence for the separated denominations and, in balance, an excessive harshness towards Catholicism. 'Charity is absent nowhere. Should we say it seems almost too kind?', asked the Swiss ecclesiologist

---

105. Undated letter (summer 1937), Congar papers. The *imprimatur* was given on 22 June, and the book, with the sub-title *Principes d'un 'œcuménisme' catholique*, was published in July of that year.

106. Étienne Fouilloux, *Les catholiques et l'unité chrétienne du XIXᵉ au XXᵉ siècle. Itinéraires européens d'expression française* (Paris: Le Centurion, 1982), 238–241; 434–445. The review in the Barthian journal *Foi et vie* 'quite clearly illustrates . . . the dangerous nature' of the book, Labourdette wrote to Nicolas on 17 October 1938.

107. Review dated 15 September 1937, along with an even harsher letter from the author, the convert CG Mortimer, dated 15 October, Congar papers.

Charles Journet, a close friend of Jacques Maritain.[108] The
only truly dissonant note was the review by Nicolas,
professor of theology at the Institut catholique de
Toulouse, who emphasised this complaint. Of course, he
first drew attention to the richness of *Chrétiens désunis*,
while expressing astonishment at the young Congar's
boldness on a complex subject in which 'the old masters
advanced with more fear and doubt'. Further on he
developed two basic objections. The religious experience
of the 'dissidents', whatever its value, had to be measured
against objective truth; subjectivism and relativism lay
in wait for anyone who ignored this cardinal truth. The
Catholic Church had lost nothing substantial in its battle
against heresy and schism, so to insinuate the opposite
was not only to incriminate the work completed since
the Council of Trent, but to undermine its marks of
Catholicity and holiness.[109]

Nicolas rightly felt that his criticism could damage
Congar, and so had sent the draft to his friend
Labourdette. Having taken the advice of Paul Philippe,
now in the post at the Angelicum having been at Le
Saulchoir, Labourdette encouraged Nicolas to go ahead.
'You can conveniently veil some of your over-strong
praise and mention the criticism you want to, which is
fair; I do understand your feelings but the trend is too
dangerous for us to let it pass without criticism. And if
we do not defend theological thought, who will?'[110] The
two Toulouse Dominicans soon learned that their wish

---

108. *Nova et vetera* (July-September 1938): 346–448 at 346;
     however he would find many passages in Nicolas' review
     'rather harsh'; letter from Labourdette to Nicolas, 29 July
     1938, ADT.
109. *Revue thomiste,* 44 (1938): 381–390 at 381.
110. Letter dated 31 December 1937, ADT.

anticipated that of Garrigou-Lagrange. 'I wonder whether Fr Congar's book–he is brilliant and alert–is really safe. When one is still young it is very difficult to make a precise and firm judgement on such difficult, varied, complex subjects, and that also presupposes a very broad and serious competence. There are good things there, but I fear that there is also excess', wrote Garrigou-Lagrange to Labourdette; Labourdette added, 'For me, Fr Chenu's manifesto . . . persuades me that we must absolutely fight this idea of systems and of religious experience.'[111] Congar and Chenu, the same battle. 'I have sent Fr Rosaire a draft of your review', Labourdette wrote to Nicolas, 'and he is as enthusiastic about this admirable writing as Fr Browne, Fr Garrigou, the Frs Philippe'.[112] Congar knew nothing of this correspondence, which enables us to better understand the formulation of the grievances brought against him in January 1939. As soon as Nicolas' review was published, however, he scented danger and, without much success, sought to set up a counter-attack. He obtained nothing from Cardinal Verdier whom he had known as his superior at the Carmelite seminary, and even less from Cardinal Baudrillart, whom he met on 2 May and seemed to be ill-disposed towards the Dominicans.[113] As for Cardinal Tisserant, Louis advised him not to appeal to him in the letter which also passed

---

111. Letter to Nicolas, 14 January 1938, ADT.

112. Letter dated 6 April 1938. Rosaire is Marie-Rosaire Gagnebet, of the Toulouse Province, a professor at the Angelicum; the Philippes are Paul Philippe and Thomas Philippe, professors at the Angelicum who had previously been at Le Saulchoir; Fr Vosté wrongly attributed the lineage of Nicolas' review to Garrigou-Lagrange in a letter to Congar dated 28 May.

113. Note of the audience, 11 hand-written pages.

on Gillet's refusal:[114] the Master General 'cannot commit his signature and his authority to the approval of a series or a book in a collection which must inspire respect through its academic value, and while waiting for this, is subject to discussion'. '*Privately*, however, I can tell you and I ask you to say this to Fr Congar, I am delighted to see the activity of our Fathers who are engaged in studies of such importance, and who are asserting themselves with authority', Gillet wrote to Chenu on 30 May 1938. Although these studies were renewing 'a host of questions which are extremely current', he could not support them '*publicly*', although he reserved the right to defend them if necessary 'against unfair interpretations or summary judgements made in the name of these "routines" which you have rightly denounced, and that "static" mind-set which is the enemy a priori of any dynamism and every legitimate development'. Such support reassured Chenu and Congar, who heard nothing more about it until Gillet's letter to Chenu dated 17 January 1939, which included a new list of five points.

> Errors which reappear today, following an imprudent confusion between *Christian faith* and *religious experience*. In several recent works and articles we find the equivalent[115] of the following propositions:

---

114. 'We also found, rightly, that it [*Chrétiens désunis*] would have benefitted from certain doctrinal parts being more developed', the Master General's socius wrote to Congar on 26 May 1938.

115. 'You can guess which trial is hidden under that "equivalent", Chenu wrote to Fr Henri-Dominique Gardeil, a professor at Le Saulchoir and the nephew of Ambroise Gardeil, on 28 February 1939.

1) *Christian faith is the shared religious experience of Christians*, an experience of *the value of the Christian life and the demands* of the Mystical Body of Christ, which must always be perfected according to the needs of the times, *rather than adherence* to the dogmatic formulas proposed by the Church *propter auctoritatem Dei revelantis*.

2) This is why when individual religious experience deviates and falls into error it must be *corrected* by the criteria of the *shared religious experience of authentic Christians*, which is something which is always living, full, and which renews everything according to the needs of the times, rather than through the dogmatic formulas which are always a partial, incomplete expression of this shared religious experience, and often too hard and rigid.

3) *Dogmatic formulas*, although true and always maintaining the same meaning, *always remain relative*, in a dual metaphysical and historical relativity. They are thus always imperfect and so 'radically fragile' that they are *relatively true*, rather than absolutely true.

4) *Dogmatic formulas are 'a conceptualisation of religious experience'* or a way of expressing that living and complete experience through fixed and always defective concepts.

5) *The religious experience of Protestants*, while deficient and containing many errors, *conserves aspects and tendencies of the true Christian life, particular tendencies which are found in a less living manner in the Catholic Church*. Through the conversion of Protestants, the Catholic Church would become not only quantitively, *but also qualitatively richer and more Catholic*.

In light of this document it is difficult to understand why
the accompanying letter from Gillet targets Congar and
Chrétiens désunis, since the first four points, even though
an approximation or in forced terms, target Chenu's phrase
on theology as spirituality having found the rational tools
of its religious experience, a phrase which he retracted
in Rome in February 1938. Nearly a year later, then, the
matter was not finished. Only the fifth point, by hardening
it, targets a major theme of Congar's ecumenism, already
criticised by Nicolas. Gillet intervened 'to tell you of
and soften certain *warnings* which might be made in
higher places, if necessary, under the pressure of certain
theologians who [. . .] regret the confusion in some pages
which would benefit from being corrected.'[116] Plainly this
was a decision by the Holy Office, to which the book
had probably been referred. 'Fr Congar is rebuked for
appealing for the test of faith to be more about *religious
experience* than the Church's definitions and dogmatic
formulas': a rebuke without foundation in these terms,
but which he shared with his friend and mentor, Chenu.
The Master General suggested to him that he write a
letter stating that he 'had never wished to question nor
weaken anything of the Church's Magisterium; and
that in addressing himself particularly to our separated
brethren, he emphasise what might convince them the
most', and that he was prepared to make the corrections
recommended to him in a second edition. Equipped with
this 'lightening conductor', Gillet could see off 'the storm
if it were ever to threaten this wonderful work.' He knew

---

116. Pages 34, 35 (unilateral hardening of the Catholic
position), 50, *52* (the originally correct spiritual intention
of the dissidents), 316, 319, 320 (elements in the dissidents'
position missing in Catholicisty), 330 (return to the
sources), Gillet indicated to him.

of nothing official, 'or even unofficial', but he thought he could 'guess at some concerns', and thus he had taken the initiative.[117]

Chenu responded that he had no doubt that Congar would submit to this process on his return to Le Saulchoir; he was currently preaching at Lyon for the 'octave of prayers for the Unity of the Church', where he had been invited by Fr Paul Couturier. Chenu was also sorry about the way in which, in *Chrétiens désunis*, the 'doctrinal elements' whose synthesis—'Church, mystical body and institutional magisterium, knowledge of faith and doctrinal formulas'—Congar had explained had been split up. Still scalded by his own recent misadventure, he concluded that 'there is no worse way to treat a thought than to "chop it into pieces"'.[118] Having discussed it with Journet and Nicolas, Congar beat a retreat on the five incriminating points: the hardening of the Catholic positions after the Reform only concerned the work of theologians, not the church's faith; what there was of truth in Luther's spiritual attitude only concerned his life as a religious before his split with Rome; besides, emphasising a spiritual current neither minimises the role of the teaching church nor the dogmas the church defines; he had 'never had made religious experience, individual or collective, a criteria for faith'; but he maintained that there existed forms of spiritual experience among the dissidents which

---

117. Letter to Chenu dated 17 January 1939. Alors que *Gregorianum*, While the journal of the Gregorian university, *Gregorianum*, published a favourable review by Fr Pierre Chaillet, Paul Philippe thought he knew that 'two Jesuit fathers complained about the book and may have denounced it', his letter quoted in a letter from Labourdette to Nicolas, 31 December 1937, ADT.

118. Copy of a letter to Gillet, wrongly dated 17 January.

were less present than within Catholicism; the possible expansion of Catholicity did not concern its substance, only its topicality. Having said this, he did regret that 'some people' had read his book in a particular 'context' which he did not clarify, but from which we can guess that he meant the proceedings against Chenu's account of the theological method at Le Saulchoir. Above all, he rejected 'the proceedings which consist in giving to a thought, 1st, a past history and a lineage, and 2nd, a context, and then in extracting from the work "propositions" which are ripped from their actual bindings and made to bear the absolute of a given idea'. In this way 'we can make an author say many things which he has not thought'. Now this was of course the practice of the Roman censors. If he were mistaken, Congar would be ready to correct himself, on condition that his critics were not made indirectly and in his absence, but directly, like the critiques of Journet and Nicolas.[119] Congar did indeed want to make amends, but not at any cost. Passing through Geneva in January 1939, he asked Journet to intervene on his behalf with Garrigou-Lagrange. 'You can tell Fr Congar that on the rare occasions I have discussed his book, I have spoken as I did in the R[evue]. Th[omiste] in April 1938, mentioning the work's good qualities, saying that he has done good, but noting too that some pages, which you yourself have noted, should have been corrected and focused before publication, and that I hope that such corrections will be made in the next edition', replied Garrigou.[120] His action:

---

119. Copy of a letter to Fr Gillet, dated 26 January.

120. Letter to Journet, dated 7 February 1939, published in volume II of *Correspondance Journet Maritain* (1930–1939) (Fribourg/Paris, 1997), 790. Congar's papers include two letters from Journet on this matter.

Nicolas' review was indeed the evidence used in Rome against *Chrétiens désunis*.

The sting of the reminder was enough for Chenu to revisit, not without a wrench, several editorial decisions taken by him or his team, in particular the articles in the *Dictionnaire de théologie catholique* on 'Thomisme' and 'Thomas d'Aquin', which were to have showcased the historical methodology of Le Saulchoir. At the request of Mgr Amann, the editor of the *Dictionnaire*, however, Chenu agreed to keep the latter article.[121] 'I really do understand your state of mind, but you have to stiffen up, *not be beaten*', was how Amann, who had been removed from his position as a science teacher at the major seminary in Nancy in 1907, wrote to him in thanks. Gillet, on the other hand, congratulated Chenu for taking these prudent steps, confirming that '*higher up* they are anxious, they are in fear of a return to Modernism. Complaints and fears on the matter are ever-increasing. There are credible rumours that the Dominicans are divided, with the younger fathers abandoning Thomist positions, wanting to modernise philosophy, theology, dogma and ... St Thomas himself of course; that positive theology must supplant speculative theology, the problem must expel scholasticism ...'. He gave the impression that 'warnings, judgements, condemnations' were possible.[122] Summoned by the Master General while he was passing through Paris on 27 and 28 April 1939, Congar learned from him that *Chrétiens désunis* had indeed been denounced and submitted to the Holy Office, but that the explanations in his letter had satisfied the censors.

---

121. Draft of Chenu's letter of 21 January 1939, and pained reply from Amman dated 29 January; see too draft of letter to Henri-Dominique Gardeil dated 28 February.

122. Letter wrongly dated 2 January (actually February) 1939.

'When Fr Garrigou read it, he said to me, "But it's perfect! After this there will be no further difficulty". Although the Master General confirmed that no Dominican had been involved in the enquiry about his book, and that Garrigou-Lagrange had not been involved, the latter's hostility remained an obsessive fear for the theologians at Le Saulchoir, as it did for those at Saint-Maximin who were close to Jacques Maritain.[123] As no-one wanted to review the new edition of his treatise *De Deo*, 'I myself did it', wrote Chenu, 'and I sent him my review. I corrected an expression where I had sought to be friendly but which he interpreted as a criticism of the "old hands".[124]

5.2. Charlier and Theological Method

'I presume that the incident with Charlier (Louvain) is at the origin of this new rise' in suspicion, wrote Chenu on 28 February 1939.[125] Towards the end of 1938, Congar too had intervened in a major debate on the definition of theology, fed by a book by his confrere Louis Charlier, *Essai sur le problème théologique*. Born in 1898, Charlier had entered the Belgian Province of the Dominicans in 1915; ordained priest in 1922 he had taught theology and the history of dogmas at the house of studies in Louvain since 1925. He had known Chenu for many years and followed his publications with keen interest. On 22 January 1938, he thanked Chenu for having sent his 'wonderful manifesto', writing,

---

123. Typed, signed note, undated; letter from Labourdette to Nicolas on 17 March 1939, very harsh about Garrigou, ADT.

124. Draft of a letter to Henri-Dominique Gardeil; in *Bulletin thomiste* (Oct-Dec 1937): 535–538.

125. Letter quoted to Henri-Dominique Gardeil.

> This is how I allow myself to refer to *Une école de théologie Le Saulchoir*. I have read and re-read it with a *very special* interest because your words respond precisely to the preoccupations of my personal reflection. I am pleased to feel myself so fully in communion 'of mind-set' with you. I am in the midst of finishing off the publication of my notes on the problem of theology. Fr Provincial forces me to do so–he absolutely wants me to pass my *ad gradus* exam in a few months. My work suffers from its completion point–a thesis to be defended in front of a Roman jury. Hence some reticence and a certain deliberate lack of precision. I shall send you the book as soon as it is printed.

Warned by Chenu about the Roman setbacks of *Une école de théologie*,[126] Charlier was hesitant about publishing his book, but it was nonetheless published in September 1938 by a small Belgian publisher.[127] Browne wrote to him on 21 September to confirm that his *ad gradus* exam would take place on 4 November; but on 23 October, a counter-order: the religious tasked with reading *Essai sur le problème théologique* thought that there were difficulties and it should therefore be carefully examined. Just as Chenu was showing Charlier his support, rumours from Rome suggested that Charlier would not be allowed to respond to the criticisms addressed to him.[128]

---

126. Letter to Charlier dated 27 March 1938.
127. Thuillies, Ramgal, *imprimatur* dated 30 March 1938.
128. Letter from Labourdette to Nicolas dated 17 mars 1939, ADT. The Charlier question has been masterfully dealt with by Robert Guelluy, 'Les antécédents': 421–497; and more recently by Jürgen Mettepenningen, 'L'*Essai* de Louis Charlier (1938): Une contribution à la nouvelle théologie', in *Revue théologique de Louvain,* 39 (2008): 211–232, and above all in Ward De Pril's *Theological Renewal* on the Draguet affair.

Absorbed in editing his article 'Théologie' for Amman's *Dictionnaire*, Congar wrote a dispassionate state-of-the-question article for the *Bulletin thomiste* at the end of 1938,[129] in which he analysed four positions: that of Fr René Draguet, professor at the theology faculty in Louvain in three articles written for the *Revue catholique des idées et des faits*;[130] that taken by the Franciscan Jean-François Bonnefoy in a series of articles which had been reissued in a single volume;[131] the position taken by Louis Charlier's *Essai*; and finally, that of Marie-Rosaire Gagnebet, of the Toulouse Province, then assigned at the Angelicum.[132] Despite Chenu's *Une école de théologie* having initially stirred up the problem, he was omitted from this panorama, because to describe his opinion it would have been necessary to divulge the enquiry to which he had just been submitted, which was out of the question. Charlier had avoided mentioning a booklet to which he privately acknowledged he was indebted. After analysing the writings of St Thomas, the first three authors [Draguet, Bonnefoy, Charlier] had more or less firmly come down against the thesis that theology is a science in the Aristotelian sense of the term, which is capable of helping the understanding of the revealed data,

---

129. Issue October-December 1938, 490–505 (text dated November).

130. 'Méthodes théologiques d'hier et d'aujourd'hui', 10 January 1936, 1–7; 7 February, 4–7; 14 February, 13–17.

131. 'La théologie comme science et l'explication de la foi selon saint Thomas d'Aquin', in *Ephemerides theologicae lovanienses*, 14 (1937): 421–446, 600–631; 15 (1938): 491–516; *La nature de la théologie selon saint Thomas d'Aquin* (Paris: Vrin, 1939).

132. 'La nature de la théologie spéculative', in *Revue thomiste*, 44 (1938): 1–39, 213–255, 645–674.

a thesis which the commentators had unduly hardened. Bonnefoy was the most radical, but he was only a Thomist 'in passing'; then there was Draguet, a historian who denied the validity of speculative theology, to the benefit of the 'positive of the magisterium'. Charlier's discreetly reformist programme', which Congar 'politely' critiqued,[133] seemed more balanced.[134] Only Gagnebet proclaimed the classical Thomist position loud and clear. Congar quoted him at length before indicating his full agreement with a study which was 'truly blessed, precise, penetrating, and enlightening'. Like his Toulouse confrere, he professed that 'theology, applying itself to know the realities revealed by our natural means cannot be content with a method from pure authority, but must use reason to constitute a science of the revealed God, must submit itself to the logical laws of the workings of our mind, and finally, must make use of natural scientific data'.[135] With nuances since his 1927 article ('La théologie comme science au XIIIe siècle'), this position was also held by Chenu, and one which Charlier explicitly contested in his book.[136]

One might think that Congar's agreement with the classical thesis would be a credit to Le Saulchoir, but this was not the case for two reasons. First, the Charlier affair revived suspicion towards French-speaking Dominicans: Gagnebet, about whom Labourdette wrote that he would be 'like Fr Garrigou, as touchy about himself as he is harsh

---

133. Congar, in *Bulletin thomiste* (1938): 492.
134. As Chenu wrote on 30 April 1942 to the Lazarist Fr Bayol.
135. In *Bulletin thomiste* (1938): 505.
136. 'We are fearful that here [on theology as a science], Fr Gardeil's disciple in Fr Ch[enu], has got the better of the historian', *Essai sur le problème théologique,* 114, note.

towards others',[137] trounced Charlier in a lengthy review.[138] Above all, Draguet, who does not seem to have been aware of the Roman trials of *Une école de théologie*, made a link between Charlier and Chenu in his review of *Essai sur le problème théologique*. With Charlier's agreement, the review strongly emphasised the borrowings Charlier had made from the course on the subject which Draguet had given during the 1934–1935 university year; and according to Draguet, the book should be placed 'in its rightful place alongside a series of recent works which in various degrees lean in a similar direction, inspired by similar preoccupations. We are thinking in particular of the works by the Dominicans at Le Saulchoir, who not long ago expressed their guiding principles in a booklet which deserved to be widely read', with the reference in brackets.[139] The same direction? This is debatable. Robert Guelluy's conclusion, having carefully compared the three incriminating works, is more nuanced. According to him,

> the most original part of Charlier's work is his study of St Thomas, in which he separates from Chenu, and it cannot be said that he reproduces Draguet's short analysis. To deal with the inspiration of theological work, Charlier does follow in Chenu's wake. As for methods, he clearly follows Draguet: with him and Chenu, he reckons that the representatives of post-Tridentine theology hardened St Thomas' thinking, while with Draguet *contra* Chenu, he believes that Thomas did not want to make theology a 'science' in the

---

137. Letter quoted to Nicolas, 17 March 1939.

138. 'Un essai sur le problème théologique', in *Revue thomiste*, 45 (1939): 108–145.

139. In *Ephemerides theologicae lovanienses*, 16 (1939): 143–145 at 145; the *imprimatur* for this volume is dated 15 March 1939.

> Aristotelian sense of the term; with Chenu but
> *contra* Draguet, he preaches the complementarity
> of positive and speculative theology, while Draguet
> considered speculative theology to be optional, or
> at least, of very little interest.[140]

The convergences between the three theologians, whom Draguet was the first and the only one to establish a parallel between, were therefore negative rather than positive. They shared the same reservations about late scholasticism, which they saw as a degeneration of speculative theology from the end of the Middle Ages onwards, although it continued to dominate the Roman universities and dicasteries. On the other hand, 'a careful attention to the use of vocabulary' was needed to discern the links between Chenu's booklet and Charlier's essay, 'since they were so discreet'.[141] Such attention should at least prevent the second from being mapped onto the first, as Mgr Parente would do in 1942. The only piece of evidence establishing a lineage between Chenu and Charlier, Draguet's clumsy review, thus did not pass unnoticed in Rome.

5.3. The Inheritance of the Tübingen School

In spring of 1939, there was a new crisis: a decree from the Holy Office dated 20 March ordered that 'all copies' of Johann-Adam Möhler's *L'Unité dans l'Église*, published

---

140. 'Les antécédents de l'encyclique "*Humani generis*"', 451.
141. 'Les antécédents de l'encyclique "*Humani generis*"', 451. In total there are three bibliographical references in *Essai sur le problème théologique* to Chenu, all in the notes (pages 11, 34, 114), and the last of which, also the most explicit, takes the opposing view to his 1927 article, 'La théologie comme science au XIIIe siècle'.

barely a year earlier,[142] 'which are still on sale or at the publishers, must be withdrawn from circulation, their sale is forbidden as is any reprinting'.[143] The decision reached Éditions du Cerf and Congar at the start of May without any explanation. Although it concerned the distribution of the book rather than its content, it still seemed symbolic. The re-edition of *L'Unité dans l'Église*, translated by the Lilienfeld monk Amay André and with a preface by Pierre Chaillet, professor at the Jesuit scholasticate at Fourvière, the greatest French specialist on Möhler, certainly had aspects of being on trend. In 1938, the centenary of the Tübingen theologian's death led to a rediscovery of his work, led in France by Chaillet and Congar. But there was more. Only material shortages had prevented *L'Unité dans l'Église* from being the first in the '*Unam Sanctam*' series, whose entry-point and model it should have been. Published in 1825, this youthful work whose author, 'aware of its imperfections' had refused to re-publish, 'is still a powerful stimulus for us today', as Congar would later write. Möhler 'wished to abandon a purely juridical and apologetic vision of the Church as a hierarchical society and a teaching authority instituted as such by God. He viewed it starting from its internal principle, the Holy Spirit, the principle of mutual love which produced visible expressions of community life in history'.[144] The founder of the '*Unam Sanctam*'

---

142. *L'Unité dans l'Église ou le principe du Catholicisme d'après l'esprit des Pères des trois premiers siècles de l'Église*, translated by Dom A de Lilienfeld, introduction by Père Chaillet, sj, 'Unam Sanctam', 2 (Paris: Cerf, 1938).

143. Letter from Cardinal Marchetti-Selvaggiani to Cardinal Verdier dated 19 April, Prot. 15/1939, copy in the archives of the Éditions du Cerf.

144. Quotation from his article 'Möhler' in the encyclopaedia *Catholicisme*, volume IX, column 460.

series shared this conviction, wanting to use the series to 'make the nature or, as it were, the mystery of the Church, known', 'a notion of the Church which is truly rich, living, full of sap from the Bible and Tradition'.[145] The young Congar's ecclesiology was profoundly influenced by Möhler, to whom he dedicated several articles;[146] following Möhler, he sought to move the definition of the church from the institutional and hierarchical concept of an uncompromising mould towards an idea of mystery, life, and community. But Möhler had a whiff of sulphur about him, for, according to the entry about him in the *Dictionnaire de théologie catholique*, he had been considered to be 'an unwitting precursor of Catholic Modernism'.[147]

To take the decision to withdraw from sale a French re-publication of *L'Unité dans l'Église* was therefore not insignificant, even if the decision did not allude to the debate in the background. Congar had sensed the danger and kept his distance from Möhler's 'unilateralism' in a defence and description of the series.[148] Rather less harmless than Möhler was one of the prominent figures of the Tübingen school, whom Chenu explicitly claimed to follow. Having dedicated his 'Position de la théologie'

---

145. Prospectus for the series' launch.
146. 'La signification œcuménique de l'œuvre de Möhler', in *Irénikon*, 15 (1938): 113–130; 'Note sur l'évolution et l'interprétation de la pensée de Möhler', in *RSPT*, 27 (1938): 205–212; 'L'esprit des Pères d'après Möhler', in *Supplément de la Vie spirituelle* (April 1938): 1-25; 'L'hérésie, déchirement de l'unité', in *L'Église est une. Hommage à Möhler* (Paris: Bloud et Gay, 1939), 255–269.
147. 'Moehler Jean-Adam', volume 10/2, columns 2048–2063 at 2063.
148. 'Autour du renouveau de l'ecclésiologie: la collection "Unam Sanctam"', in *La Vie intellectuelle*, 61 (1939): 9–32.

to Matthias Scheeben, whom he emulated, he proudly proclaimed this inheritance in *Une École de théologie*, writing,

> Here, in its very vocabulary, is the main theme of the Catholic Tübingen theologians (Drey, Moehler). At Le Saulchoir we have been pleased to borrow from these masters of the Catholic German renaissance of the nineteenth century, at the same time as, in theology and the revelation of faith, we are similarly inspired by M. J. Scheeben. With them we reject the abstract intellectualism of the *Aufklärung* and its indifference to history: these wrongs are connected and did not avoid contaminating modern scholasticism, disingenuously reinforcing the host manuals, even the Thomist ones.[149]

More than Pascal or Newman, who could both just as well have served them in loosening the vice-like grip of scholasticism, Chenu and his disciple Congar made use of these nineteenth-century German theologians to return to the spiritual foundations of Christian faith, far removed from the abstract elaborations which had replaced it for centuries. But these theologians were themselves suspect in Rome. During their meeting in Paris on 27 April 1939, Gillet confirmed to Congar that Möhler had been denounced to the Holy Office, 'because of his tendencies in which they see a certain Modernist flavour, and because of the lack of precision of the author on the question of Roman primacy'. The outcome of

---

149. *Une école*, pages 66-67 (and page 99). From the historian's perspective the reference to the German *Aufklärung* is debatable; as the source of Romanticism the *Aufklärung* was far more sensitive to the spiritual than the French *Lumières*.

this, however, was different from that which the Master General announced then, purely internal to the Order.[150]

Congar drew up two explanatory documents for the archdiocese of Paris which were to give an account to the Holy Office of how the measures had been applied, including press reviews, favourable no doubt[151] and some defensive comments. Möhler being 'a well-known theologian, we did not see why a French version of his book would encounter difficulties which the German re-publication did not meet', that edition having been published in 1925 to mark the centenary. Of course, Möhler 'did not express himself very clearly on the question of the primacy of the Pope', which Chaillet had emphasised in his preface along with other weaknesses in the work. 'As for the suspicion of a pre-Modernist flavour', this was in Congar's eyes 'unjustified', and here he took refuge behind the authority of the Jesuit Léonce de Grandmaison. The 'anonymous persecution' which 'one of the works of theology which most marked the Catholic restoration of the nineteenth century' was subjected to, seemed unjustifiable to him, without Mgr Dupanloup and Cardinal Newman 'who went further than Möhler', also being condemned. Congar was protesting against a measure which in his view should be softened or even withdrawn.[152]

And Congar was not alone in his opinion. The philosopher Étienne Borne indicated that Francisque Gay was anxious, for *Hommage à Möhler*, edited by Chaillet,

---

150. Conagr, letter to Fr Dupin, Vicar General of Paris with responsibility for granting *imprimatur*, 7 May.

151. 'Extraits de presse au sujet de la traduction française du livre de Möhler', 2 typed pages.

152. 'Remarques au sujet de "L'Unité dans l'Église" de Möhler', 2 typed pages.

was in production and risked a similar fate.[153] Likewise the
Christian Democrat Georges Bidault wondered whether
an intervention by the French embassy to the Holy See
was desirable.[154] For his part, Congar wrote to Georges
Goyau, known for his work on the religious history of
nineteenth-century Germany. 'As a reaction against the
Reformation, the Aufklärung, and Febronism, *Unity in
the Church* marked a renewal of the idea of the Church
on the German side of the Rhine', Goyau, a member of
the Académie française, wrote to Gillet, who had his
letter read to Pius XII. Forbidding its French translation,
therefore, was a nonsense.[155] Against all the evidence,
the Master General confirmed that the decree changed
nothing in terms of the instructions issued to Paris at
the end of April. 'Do not give more importance to this
matter by letting it get out; it's annoying, but that's all', he
wrote to Chenu on 11 May. Refuting every 'manœuvre'
against Le Saulchoir, he hoped to see it continue with its
'magnificent work' and 'to take account of these *very minor
irritations* only in order to avoid more serious ones.'[156] He
suggested simply that Congar, who was about to publish
Fr Gratieux' thesis on the Slavophile Khomiakov, distance
himself from the 'doctrines of the Russians'.[157] The report

---

153. *L'Église est une. Hommage à Möhler*; Renée Bédarida,
Pierre Chaillet. Témoin de la résistance spirituelle (Paris:
Fayard, 1988), 39–73.

154. Letter from Étienne Borne to 'Dear Father and friend', 7
May, Éditions du Cerf archives.

155. Letter to Congar dated 9 May.

156. Similar recommendations in his letter to Congar dated 15
May.

157. Letter to Chenu dated 11 May. Albert Gratieux, *A. S.
Khomiakov et le Mouvement Slavophile*, '*Unam Sanctam*' 5
and 6, *nihil obstat* from Congar, 1 April 1939, *imprimatur*
from Dupin, 3 April.

from the vicar general, Dupin, conformed to Congar's wish, indicating that the centenary had given rise to many tributes to Möhler, in both books and journals. He emphasised that the new edition had received the *nihil obstat* from a Master of Sacred Theology, Chenu. In particular, he explained that a book published forty-five years before the [First] Vatican Council could not take the dogmatic conclusions of that Council into account, and that Chaillet had clarified this in his introduction, both in terms of the accusation of pre-Modernism and of the role of the papacy, with lengthy supporting citations. In granting his *imprimatur*, therefore, the archbishop of Paris had hardly been lacking in prudence.[158]

'There is no example of the Holy Office withdrawing a *decree*', wrote Gillet.[159] He was quickly proved wrong, as even though the measure had not been made public, it was withdrawn following a political intervention at the highest level. 'Some ten days ago, I asked the President of the Council to intervene about the Moehler business', Bernadot, founder and director of the Éditions du Cerf wrote to Congar on 16 May.

> They have exhausted the Vatican schemes; it was agreed with the leader of Daladier's cabinet that they would say that they would not tolerate French Catholics being treated in this way and that by bullying some sections of French Catholicism, they are permitting the Catholic press to repeat its tone from 30 years ago. Now, Fr B[ernadot] tells me that the step has been taken, and a moment ago I was told that a coded dispatch, which arrived at 18h, announced that the Holy Office's decree has

---

158. Report of 5 typed pages, attached to his letter to Congar dated 11 May.

159. Letter to Congar dated 15 May.

been withdrawn. I considered that there was no doctrinal issue there, since the German edition had been permitted; but that this was the follow-up to the battle led by those who wish to destroy this house [. . .] Considering that I was meddling in Church politics, and that the Church was acting politically in this matter, I acted by the same means and had no hesitation in having recourse, not to the Foreign Office and Canet, but directly to the President of the Council. 'We have had enough of these Roman processes', added Bernadot, also noting his lack of confidence in Pius XII.[160]

Congar's unedited journal confirms this—the matter was dealt with by 'Monsieur Chastaignau', almost certainly Yves Chataigneau, general secretary to the President of the Council,[161] and there was little delay, as a telegram from the ambassador to the Holy See, François Charles-Roux, announced the happy ending on 16 May. 'And this is how the Church is really governed', commented Bernadot. 'If the government had not taken up our defence, we would once again have been denounced to French Catholics as a suspect house. The Government is angry, silence. Yet they acted, they say, out of doctrine.'[162]

I have two observations on this surprising epilogue. For the Dominicans of the Éditions du Cerf, this was discreet revenge, after the suppression of *Sept* and the threats towards *La Vie Intellectuelle*. And it confirms the good intentions of Édouard Daladier's 'national unity' government towards French Catholicism: one cannot imagine Bernadot taking such steps towards the government of the Front Populaire. Cardinal Verdier,

---

160. Congar's hand-written note about the meeting.

161. Unedited journal, 6 May, sent by Fr André Duval, ADF.

162. Unedited journal, 16 May.

whom Congar found to have the same tendency as
Bernadot on 17 May, nonetheless refused to write a
congratulatory letter to Fr Gratieux for *Khomiakov*,
convinced that such a letter would bring the same wrath
on his head as it would on Gratieux, although this turned
out not to happen.[163] On the other hand, his auxiliary,
Mgr Beaussart wrote to Chenu to express how much
he expected from St Dominic's Order.[164] Roman ways
remained decidedly impenetrable: while the first two
volumes of the '*Unam Sanctam*' series were tried by
the Holy Office, the good offices of Fr Paolo Manna, an
Italian missionary and missiologist, offered their editor
the possibility of defending the series in *L'Osservatore
Romano*, at the start of July 1939.[165]

5.4. Cordovani and Boyer

And then the war began, which noticeably slowed work at
Le Saulchoir down, as some students and professors were
mobilised, including Congar, who was taken prisoner in
June 1940.[166] But for 'the defenders of eternal truths, war is
an earthly epiphenomenon which does not interrupt their
holy work', noted Chenu with irony, now anxious about
two new attacks.[167] On 14 March 1940, at the Angelicum,

---

163. Hand-written note about the audience.
164. In the new circumstances of war, letter dated 9 November
      1939.
165. YC. 'Una serie di pubblicazioni sulla Chiesa. La collezione
      "*Unam Sanctam*"', 7 July 1939.
166. There were 136 students for the 1938–1939 academic year,
      including 24 La Salette Religious, and 61 for the academic
      year 1941–1942 (not including the La Salette students).
      Reports in AGOP XIII 30200/2.
167. Letter to Motte dated 5 November 1940, ADF.

Fr Mariano Cordovani gave a lecture on theology for the
annual feast in honour of St Thomas, which *L'Osservatore
Romano* broadly echoed in its 22 March issue, and which
was later published in the college review. The first part
defined theology in a classical manner, as the rational
approach of faith founded on the sources of Revelation and
on Thomist thought, which had been given new prestige
by the popes from Leo XIII onwards. The second part,
entitled 'on some modern tendencies' started by attacking
the temptation of 'subjectivism' which presented dogma,
not as a revealed truth, 'but as the religious experience
of the faithful', and the hierarchy of the Church not as
divinely instituted but as 'a conceptualisation of the life
of love lived in common'. It is difficult not to link these
with some of the formulas for which Chenu had been
chastised. Cordovani, Master of the Apostolic Palace,
then attacked the '*studiosi*' who denigrated the church's
past and respected nothing, 'not even St Thomas Aquinas'.
This dual 'psychological and historical relativism' was
invading books which were presented as 'programmes
for reform'. Some authors suggested theology was born
of 'free and audacious contemplation', whose single and
immediate source was 'the current experience of religious
life' and did not recoil from the idea of 'creative tradition'.
Here Cordovani was emphasising the effect of such an
approach on the understanding of the Church as the
mystical body of Christ, following Scheeben, whom he
described as 'theologically straying', but without citing
Möhler. The encyclical *Mystici Corporis Christi* would
put the dots on the 'I's in 1943. According to Cordovani,
the same fault could also be found in the similar question
of 'the union of dissidents with Holy Mother Church',
through 'over-valuing Russian Christianity', particularly
the statement that the 'schism possess something
missing' in the Catholic Church, or where the Catholic

Church's dogmatic definitions 'impoverish and harden revealed truth'. Here it is difficult not to see some of the criticisms recently made about Congar's ecumenism.[168] Yet Cordovani believed in the freedom of academic work and said he did not approve of the 'passion for the hunt which goes in search of someone's errors for the slight satisfaction of pointing out the errors of a colleague working in the same theological citadel'.[169] Warned by Gillet, Chenu clearly understood that the point of Cordovani's lecture 'was deliberately directed (with no names) against Fr Congar and [him]'. But 'until I hear to the contrary', he felt that this was more 'a return to the "past", not a new stage in the 1938 incidents. If I'm wrong – beware!'[170]

Shortly afterwards, Fr Charles Boyer, a Jesuit from the Toulouse Province then in a post at the Gregorian university offered measured 'Réflexions sur une controverse', entitled, 'Qu'est-ce que la théologie?' His account, close in spirit to Congar's in the *Bulletin thomiste*, reviewed the positions of Draguet, Charlier, Bonnefoy, and Gagnebet, attacking Charlier in particular on three main points. First, the role of philosophical reason in theology, which Charlier had incorrectly reduced, according to Boyer: if the truths of faith could not be proved by reason, either 'dogmas will be emptied of meaning, or reason blind', he wrote. Here he contested Charlier's reading of St Thomas' thinking on the matter, 'absolutely clear and very much in favour of rational speculation in theology'. Finally, he feared that

---

168. A final paragraph deals with those who support inverting the ends of marriage so that conjugal love precedes welcoming children.

169. 'Per la vitalità della teologia cattolica', in *Angelicum* 17 (1940): 132–146 at 141–144.

170. Letter to Motte dated 5 November 1940.

the displacement of theology as the science of the living magisterium of the church, as proposed by Draguet and Charlier, would end in 'new statements, which would be difficult to accept', for tradition could only be 'the explanation of truths contained in some way, formal or virtual', in the revealed data which closed with the death of the last apostle. 'It is not what is revealed which develops and grows, but only the knowledge of what is revealed'. Following Congar, he indicated his substantial agreement with Gagnebet and defined theology as 'the science whose object is to expose and study the truths which God has revealed to us about himself in their connections and their necessary consequences'.[171]

The refutation of Charlier's *Essai* was harsh, even though Boyer adopted the tone of academic debate between colleagues rather than that of the inquisitorial polemic. Le Saulchoir was almost entirely absent from the article. Of course, an initial note included 'various works' by Chenu among the contents of the file, but this was simply one reference in the midst of many others, without any discussion, a wish to 'respect the order of silence which the Dominicans had observed since 1938', suggests Robert Guelluy.[172] On the other hand, Boyer felt that Congar, 'despite some reservations, which are particularly directed towards Fr Bonnefoy, makes more than one important concession to the new interpretation of St Thomas' texts, and shows himself to be very sympathetic to Fr Charlier's work'.[173] This judgement is curious: of course, Congar had avoided criticising his Belgian colleague too heavily, but *in fine*, just as Boyer did, he had aligned

---

171. In *Gregorianum*, 21 (1940): 255–266 at 258, 259, 264, 265, 266.
172. Guelluy, 'Les antécédents', 472.
173. Guelluy, 'Les antécédents', 256.

himself with Gagnebet's 'traditional and true' position.[174] There is no further allusion to the French Dominicans in Boyer's article, but it is negative, and for the first time the criticisms came from a theologian outside of the Order.

'I have heard (but it is difficult to check) that Fr Boyer wrote his article on instructions from the highest level', worried the Spanish *socius* Emmanuel Montoto, in a letter to Gillet, now exiled in Fribourg, dated 9 August 1940. Whatever the truth, 'there is much talk in some Roman circles of the new doctrine which the Dominican fathers are teaching which is against the tradition of the Order', he added hammering Charlier: his attack on 'the strength of reason in theology' would lead to 'conclusions which are academically false and dangerous with regard to the Church's teachings'. If an intervention from on high were proven, it would justify the sending of an apostolic visitor to Belgium, France, Britain, and Canada, 'for these are the provinces whose Fathers are accused of a dangerous doctrinal freedom'.[175] There was such anxiety that Montoto touched on the words of Pius XII during his audience on 3 September: '*Nessuno Mi ha parlato mai contro l'Ordine, mai, mai*', the pope was said to have responded, unmoved by Boyer's article, '*molto tomista*'. Gillet's assistant drew from this audience that no 'higher, that is, apostolic authority' had intervened, otherwise the pope would have known about it. However he did send the article to Gillet, clarifying that Boyer was no longer in Rome, but a refugee in France.[176] The mechanism which would end in sanctions does not appear to have been engaged at the start of September 1940.

---

174. Guelluy, 'Les antécédents', 266.

175. AGOP V 305.

176. 'No one has ever spoken to me against the Order, never, never', letter dated 3 September, AGOP V 305.

The same cannot be said of January 1942, if we read correctly Gillet's reaction to the announcement that Le Saulchoir was also giving up the article 'Thomas d'Aquin' in the *Dictionnaire de théologie catholique*, unless the Master General himself would stand as guarantor for the work then taking place in the house, which was out of the question.[177] Warned without clarification by Louis and Motte[178] that the house remained under suspicion, Chenu had warned Amann of his decision, and had sent it to Gillet. 'I sense that this is a declaration of war on Le Saulchoir . . . in an interpretation of St Thomas' doctrine which has already raised such suspicion *here* and is violently opposed to some points of contemporary, so-called 'traditional' interpretation', wrote the outraged Master General, surprised by Amman's request. The same applied to 'the Order's doctrinal reputation. For that is what is at stake *here* not only at the "Angelicum" but "higher still". I cannot say any more.' Less than a fortnight before the Holy Office decree, the allusion is clear: an enquiry is about to end. 'Le Saulchoir is considered suspect of doctrinal dissidence, as the enemy, not of St Thomas, but of scholasticism, favouring certain modern ideas which are still impregnated with "Modernism"', Gillet explained, wrongly persuaded that the debate was

---

177. Letter from Amann to Cardinal Tisserant, 19 January 1942. In the published article only Spicq's section on 'Saint Thomas exégète' (vol. 15/1, columns 694–738) remained from Le Saulchoir, the main part being entrusted to five professors from the Angelicum (Walz, Gagnebet, Garrigou-Lagrange, Gillon and Geenen, columns 618–761).

178. Antonin Motte, Prior of Le Saulchoir, whose problems he was therefore very familiar with, had been elected French Provincial at the Chapter of October 1938, to replace the late Fr Padé.

more of a technicality than a trial. 'Personally I think that
it is less the ideas which you defend which have brought
you trouble, than the trenchant and dogmatic tone in
which you defend them, and the sort of scorn, irony,
and mockery with which you attack your "opponents"
who describe themselves as traditionalists', he explained,
minimising the differences. Gillet emphasised that,

> Fr Congar's book further increased this impression.
> Charlier's, approved by the Revue des Sciences
> Th[éologiques] et Ph[ilosophiques] crowned
> the emotion of official circles and others, and
> in '*Gregorianum*' Fr Boyer, from the Gregorian,
> echoed this feeling. Analysing Fr Charlier's book, he
> demonstrated dispassionately that this thesis was in
> contradiction not only with Thomism but with clear
> texts by St Thomas. It seemed surprising that it was
> a J[esuit] who took up the defence of St Th[omas],
> or orthodoxy against the sons of St Dom[inic].
> For he quoted in a note the names of those who
> had dealt with the question in a similar spirit: Frs
> Gardeil, Chenu, Congar, Marin-Sola, Rabeau.[179]

In retrospect, one can only think that this is a cryptic
summary of the matter: Charlier, then Boyer against
Charlier and, by extension, against Chenu and his
brethren, even if Boyer only criticised Congar's leniency
towards Charlier.

Did Chenu understand the message? We may well ask,
for in addition to the factual errors,[180] he particularly took

---

179. Wrong interpretation of Boyer's bibliographical note, letter
    to Chenu dated 27 January.
180. Fr Congar had reviewed Charlier's book for the *Bulletin
    thomiste*, not the *RSPT*; the intellectual lineage of the
    matter Boyer offered was wrong, as Chenu only recognised
    Ambroise Gardeil and Pierre Mandonnet as his masters.

on board his superior's 'paternal affection' and 'ongoing confidence'. 'Most Reverend Father, save our spiritual freedom for good work', he wrote, having denied any doctrinal deviation and reduced the matter to an old 'trial of tendencies' instigated against Le Saulchoir by a Roman theological school attempting to impose its methodology under cover of the authority of the magisterium. 'I hope that you are able to read between the lines of what I have written and what I cannot write, if only that this is a situation of extreme seriousness, which has the potential to compromise the interests dearest to you, and which I, like you, appreciate', Gillet wrote. This was as much a warning as the secret of the Holy Office would allow him to give Chenu of the imminent storm, unless his junior's response would 'calm them' and 'give them hope'. This was not to be the case. The response was dated 13 February 1942, more than a week after the decree which placed *Une école de théologie* on the Index, which Chenu still knew nothing about.

Chapter III
The Sanctioning Of Le Saulchior
(1942–1943)

1. The Reasons Adduced for the Condemnation

Dated 4 February 1945, ratified by Pius XII the following day, and made public the day after that, the Holy Office decree which censured Chenu's booklet and Charlier's book was published in the *Acta Apostolicae Sedis* on 24 February and in *La Croix* on 26th.[1] The highest authority has no need to justify its decisions; however there was a custom that one of its members was entrusted with the job of explaining the reason for the decision in an official way in *L'Osservatore Romano*. In this case, the lot fell on Mgr Pietro Parente, professor of theology at the pontifical colleges of the Lateran and Propaganda, and recently appointed consultor to the Holy Office. Published in Italian in the daily Vatican edition of 9-10 February, and then in Latin in the specialist Gregorian periodical *Periodica de re morali canonica liturgica*,[2] his article, entitled '*Nuove tendenze teologiche*',[3] subsequently

---

1. Page 37.
2. 31 (1942): 184–188.
3. [English translation from Patricia Kelly, *Ressourcement theology: a sourcebook* (London: Bloomsbury/T&T Clark, 2021), 85–87.]

had a wide impact, because it included the expression '*nouvelle théologie*' for the first time, an expression which became famous following Pius XII's use of it in 1946. In this article we find the five main complaints advanced against Chenu and Charlier since 1938, by both their confreres at the Angelicum and by Frs Cordovani and Boyer: a misjudgement of Modernism and its importance; philosophical and theological relativism denigrating Thomism; relativism which extended to the dogmatic formulas themselves; an erroneous definition of theology on the subjective foundation of religious experience; and finally, an exaggerated trust in history in the development of the Church's tradition.

Significantly, Parente located the authors whose censuring he was commenting on in the lineage of those who held scholastic Thomism in contempt–Laberthonnière, Loisy, and Le Roy–formerly condemned for their 'invectives' regarding Thomism. This classic procedure consisted of justifying new sanctions by assimilating them to an earlier, proscribed heresy. In this view, the fact that the Thomists Charlier and Chenu had few points in common with the 'currents of theological thinking, which have their beginnings in the Modernist lobby' had little importance. Equally wrongly, Parente associated Charlier with Chenu in the 'school of Le Saulchoir', marked by Gardeil, Lemonnyer, and Mandonnet, although Charlier had never studied nor taught there, and had explicitly distanced himself from Gardeil on the scientific nature of theology. Despite their 'best intentions', a 'lively temperament', 'love of novelty', and 'juvenile audacity' had led them to sketch out a 'reform of the theological terrain', which was not completely without merit but which was 'infected with many dangerous principles, which lend themselves to real deviation from orthodox doctrine'. The sanctioning by the Holy Office should therefore not be a surprise to anyone who had read the two offending texts, as well as the critiques by 'capable theologians' such as Boyer and Gagnebet. Objection: these two authors had only criticised Charlier, not Chenu. Response to the objection: Charlier 'followed the riskiness of certain of Chenu's original theories and went even further'. The trend was well proven.

Several major deviations—or supposed deviations— were picked up. Chenu and Charlier 'bring discredit on scholastic theology, on its speculative nature, its method, the value of its conclusions, which proceed from the data of revelation; this discredit naturally also falls on St Thomas'. Parente then assailed the relativism on dogmatic formulas attributed to the two Dominicans, particularly Charlier, whence a depreciation of reason for the benefit of sentiment and religious experience, 'which reminds one of Möhler's theories, later updated and exaggerated by the Modernists'. The lineage of earlier critics was thus validated – from Möhler to Modernism, and thence to the accused authors. Chenu, and even more so Charlier, were professing 'unaaceptable' ideas about the development of revelation which, far from being closed with the death of the last apostle, continued to grow under the influence of the church's magisterium, a position which had been excluded by the First Vatican Council and in the 1907 encyclical, *Pascendi*, written against Modernism. Furthermore, Chenu and Charlier should be deplored, said Parente, for devaluing proofs through Scripture and Tradition, to the advantage of the ecclesial Magisterium. In short, the two 'champions' of *nouvelle théologie* (italicised and in French in the original) were destroying the basis of the scholastic system then in force without the reconstruction which they proposed offering any guarantees from the perspective of orthodox belief.

Of course, the Catholic theologian should not allow himself to harden in his old-fashioned positions, 'but no new tendencies, no critiques, no demands for modern thought' could ever allow him 'to damage or to change the principal lines of the immutable truth revealed by God, guarded, interpreted, and defined by the infallible Magisterium of the Church'.

Of course, such a summary of the criticisms which had been recurring since 1938 did not in any way convince the victims, who would obtain no other justification. For Chenu, Dubarle summarised the article in nine points, to which he proposed responses borrowed from the manuals written by Garrigou-Lagrange and Billot.[4] Chenu and those close to him would incessantly emphasise the factual errors and the false genealogies and amalgams due to Parente: while it was true that expressions or ideas familiar to him could be found in his words, they had been taken out of context and made to act as unfair extrapolations. Chenu had never professed any or all of what he was accused of.

2. Reactions

2.1. The Reactions of Superiors

As an *ex officio* member of the Holy Office, the Dominican Master General must have known something about the process which had led to the sanctioning of Charlier and Chenu, but was bound by the apostolic secret. 'Of course you are aware of the painful news about Le Saulchoir', he wrote to the French Provincial, Antonin Motte, on 15 February 1942. 'I fought to the end to prevent it, but

---

4. 'Accusations by Mgr. Parente, Holy Office qualificator', 2 hand-written pages, with some annotations from Chenu.

without success', he added, plausibly. In addition to the fact that no religious superior would rejoice at seeing two of his own condemned, the close links between Gillet and Le Saulchoir, where he had taught before becoming French Provincial and then Master General, could only have added to his pain.[5] He announced to Motte an apostolic visitation in mid-March, which would personally provide him with all the details of the affair, 'with the serious personal and community consequences' it would entail for Le Saulchoir. Finally, he hoped that Chenu 'would not delay in submitting fully to the Holy Office's decree' and that Motte would make him do this as soon as possible. Louis then revealed a little more: the Holy Office's envoy would be Garrigou-Lagrange, notorious adversary of both Chenu and the direction he had imprinted on Le Saulchoir, and he would also be acting in the name of Gillet, who had 'urged him to show great charity of heart and mind'. In the meantime, Chenu was to send to the Holy Office a formal letter of submission to the measures against him: the agreement which he had sent to the Master General on 27 February would not suffice.[6]

It was not until 17 March that Gillet communicated to Chenu what the apostolic secret allowed him to.[7] He

---

5. Cardinal Baudrillart took advantage of this to rather maliciously note that the matter would hamper him 'in his academic career' (Gillet gave rise to the intention of standing for the Académie française). *Les Carnets du cardinal Baudrillart*, 20 mai 1941–14 avril 1942 (critical edition established, introduced, and annotated by Paul Christophe). (Paris: Cerf, 1999), 371.

6. Letters dated 5 and 20 March, ADF

7. Letter received 30 March, with enveloped marked 'verificato per censura' and 'geöffnet OKW'.

confirmed that he had done the impossible to prevent the storm from breaking, which, he wrote, 'would have been possible without Fr Charlier's book; it is that book, in which you are so fully cited, which unleashed everything'. This was an error. There is not one reference to Chenu's booklet in Charlier's book, which was published shortly afterwards, but which erroneously substantiated the thesis said to be canonical in the French Dominican Province. Charlier was thus mainly responsible for a sanction which affected Chenu by chance, when his positions had almost nothing in common with his Belgian confrere. Yet Gillet indicated that Roman anxieties went wider. 'At heart, this is above all a warning shot', he observed. 'They fear a return to Modernism and are demonstrating their distress that it is we, the intellectual sons of St Thomas, who give the impression of such a return.' The accusation of Modernism or 'semi-Modernism' does indeed run like a red thread throughout the file. An important clarification, however: while he had been in dispute with Chenu over his conception of theology and its teaching for a long while, Garrigou-Lagrange, 'who had been absent [from Rome] for almost two years [since 1940] has nothing to do with this'. This information would be repeated by various Roman echoes of the affair.[8] While trying to console Chenu, Gillet counselled him to put on the best possible show for the Visitor so that his report would not be too negative, and in particular to convince him that his

---

8. Thus according to Gagnebet, 'the blow came from outside the Order', letter from Labourdette to Nicolas, 27 February 1942, ADT. Fr Garrigou-Lagrange only returned to Rome in December 1941, some weeks before the sanction (letter from Bernard de Chivré, from the Dominican house at Sail-les-Bains, in the Loire, where Garrigou-Lagrange had sought refuge, 27 December 1941, AGOP XIII 30010).

'attachment to the faith, to St Thomas, to scholasticism
are not fictitious, but real'. Aware of how such a message
might appear to be insulting and unfair, he immediately
added, 'I, who know what I am upholding in terms of
your faith and supernatural spirit suffer personally from
seeing you so publicly knocked down and, through you,
the house which always has the first place in my heart'.
He informed Chenu that he had to leave Le Saulchoir
where, like Garrigou Lagrange, he thought that Thomas
Philippe should replace him following the visitation,
and that Chenu 'provisionally' could no longer teach.
Despite some unfortunate phrases, the Master General
maintained his personal regard for Fr Chenu, who was
very grateful to him.[9]

On 27 February, the date on which he received Gillet's
letter dated the 15, Motte passed its contents on to Chenu.
'Here is the letter which I received from the Most Revd. Fr.
It is as you feared', a formula which corrects his account
given to Fr Gillet on the same day. 'I told Fr Chenu of the
matter myself, and he had not suspected anything'.[10] His
personal reaction was sharp:

> What a disconcerting crisis of conscience for our
> young men to see their masters, in whom they have
> confidence, suddenly treated like criminals because
> only the most unfortunate parts of their teaching
> and writings have been retained, the possible and
> perhaps dangerous ambiguities to which distant
> readers, less accustomed to the nuances of French
> and the author's style, are exposed, without taking

9. As the pencil-written draft of his reply date 7 April, sadly
   almost illegible, shows.
10. Chenu would twice later say that he had learned about
    his placing on the Index from the radio: *Un théologien en
    liberté*, 121; *L'hommage différé au père Chenu*, p. 266.

> into account the intellectual and religious contexts,
> which by nature disappear, for those closer to the
> authors and their audience.

Throwing this doubt on the validity of the process[11] led him to plead the attenuating circumstances for Chenu and particularly for Le Saulchoir, where he would be reassured to see Chenu replaced by Thomas Philippe or Thomas Deman. On 5 March his desire to preserve Le Saulchoir led him to somewhat shake up the chronology, since he wrongly stated that *Une école de théologie* had been published before the erection of the canonical faculties, which might have led to the house being saved.[12]

According to the house chronicle, the Provincial arrived at Le Saulchoir on 25 February to inform the professors, the brethren, and the clerical students. The latter were 'pained by this blow', which they had not seen coming, unlike their professors, who had had wind of the warnings of 1938 and 1939. Re-reading *Une école de théologie*, Motte felt the work to be 'vulnerable only to the extent that it is incomplete in its foundations and provocative in its lively form': its 'admirable conception of theology' did not merit any criticism in his eyes. 'I for my part shall do whatever is possible, as a private person and as a public person to lead this ray of the Truth, which interests us infinitely more than our own reputation, even beyond our own rehabilitation'. His support was thus total, even though he asked Chenu to write as clear

---

11. As we find in the Le Saulchoir house chronicle dated 25 February: Chenu's style is 'disconcerting for theologians used to the literary style of the Schools, particularly if their mother tongue was not French'.

12. Copy of Letter to Gillet, ADF.

a report as possible to respond point by point to Parente's complaints in *L'Osservatore Romano*.[13]

The Master General thus limited himself to passing on decisions in which he had had no part, and tried to comfort their main victim. While he regretted Chenu's intemperate language, the French provincial showed himself to be fundamentally in solidarity with Chenu.

2.2. Fr Chenu

Chenu learned in quick succession of his booklet being placed on the Index and his removal as Regent and Rector. Of course, he submitted without a spirit of rebellion, but he was still visibly affected. The quip made to one of his students at that very moment, 'We say an *Ave Maria* and we carry on working', does not in itself sufficiently sum up his reaction.[14] It does perhaps refer to his brief appearance before the lectors at Le Saulchoir when the news was announced: having referred to Fr Lagrange's troubles, 'he asked us to say an *Ave Maria* for him and to continue the *studium*'s theological work with probity and fidelity'.[15] Fr Henri-Charles Desroches, from the Lyon Province, then pursuing further studies at Le Saulchoir had seen 'the giant beaten down, crying, what

---

13. 'The simpler and clearer it is, the better. You are sometimes subtle and rather obscure, and this is when it is used against you', letter dated 13 March. This report does not seem to have edited. Perhaps the file of eight documents from January 1939 onwards, drawn together by Chenu and dated 'March 1942' by hand, takes its place.

14. André Duval, 'Présentation biographique de M.-D. Chenu par ses oeuvres essentielles', in *Marie-Dominique Chenu: Moyen Âge et modernité*, 17.

15. Le Saulchoir house chronicle.

can I say, howling over his hopes destroyed by this low blow'.[16] A few direct echoes from the Rector do not shine with optimism. 'May your friendly confidence soften my pain, and save me from bitterness, in spiritual freedom', he wrote on 21 February to Étienne Gilson, one of the few friends who he had warned himself, after his mother, of course.[17] The first and most moving of the fifty or so letters of condolence which he kept is Mme Chenu's reply to her son.

> My pen refuses to describe all my sorrow to you, having learned of such a great trial, such sorrow, which strikes you at the depth of your heart and, what is more painful yet, attacks Le Saulchoir itself. Yes, I will of course pray to the Lord for you, so that you keep all your calm; at such a time, when you have been so unjustly accused, you need my prayers ... These Roman theologians have got what they wanted, having already attacked you, and they were looking for an opportunity to bring you down completely (this is a matter of plotting, jealousies, doubtless, and politics too). Rather than calming their attacks the war has encouraged them to start attacking you again and what you hold most dear, in Le Saulchoir which is your life and which you love more than anything else.[18]

---

16. 'Avec Chenu, mémorial d'un magistère', in *Foi et développement* (April-June 1990): 4; similar version in *Mémoires d'un faiseur de livres* (Paris: Lieu commun, 1992), 94.

17. 'In these sad days both your letters have been a *real* strength to me. Trust in your friendship helps me to be peaceful and free in spirit, without bitterness, as I regret that my clumsiness has harmed a great cause', 7 March, in Murphy, 'Correspondance entre É. Gilson et M.-D. Chenu', 50, 53.

18. Handwritten letter, dated 'Friday', which starts, 'My poor dear boy'.

No one other than his mother could better assess the harshness of the blow received by the theologian, whose legendary optimism was not enough to limit the damage. It was indeed his own theological project for Le Saulchoir, to which he had given all his strength for the last ten years, which compromised the condemnation of the booklet in which presented his programme.

Chenu hardly needed to wait for 'the complete submission to the Holy Office's decree' demanded of him: dated 26 March, it was published in the *Acta Apostolicae Sedis* on 1 May.[19] Without rebelling, he vigorously contested Parente's officious arguments, continuing to deny any relationship between his booklet and Charlier's book. This denial returns like a leitmotiv in the file on the affair, and as we know it was essentially supported by his superiors. Such an interpretation begins by questioning the opportunity to exhume, 'in the midst of the awful drama of this war', a matter internal to the Order, which was four years old, and seemed to have been closed. It then considered the experience of the determining nature of the trial against Charlier, 'who is considered to be my "accomplice"', even though he has never been at Le Saulchoir, 'but is a disciple of Louvain and a certain theological "positivism", to drown me with him'. His book had also been 'politely' criticised by Congar in *Bulletin thomiste*. Parente's commentary was a 'caricature' embellished with errors, a real 'trial of a trend'.[20] This off-the-cuff attempt at an explanation, which postulated that 'the Charlier question really seems to have been a determining factor' appeared at once and was later

---

19. Page 148; a draft in pencil replaces it in Chenu's papers.
20. Quotations from Chenu's letter to the Lazarist Bayol, rediscovered in 1976, Chenu's papers.

incessantly repeated by Chenu and his advocates.[21] It is no longer tenable following Robert Guelluy's detailed demonstration that Charlier was dragged into the storm as a supposed follower of Chenu. For Guelluy, it is Le Saulchoir, through its Rector, which was the target, as later events would show. The instruction against Charlier's *Essai sur le problème théologique* only enabled them to relaunch a matter which had been provisionally put on hold in 1938 and to bring it to a conclusion. 'I am now certain that it is the difficulties raised by Fr Charlier's book which explain why the confidential complaint about Chenu in 1938 became a public condemnation in 1942, which did not have either L Charlier or R Draguet in mind, but M.-D. Chenu's Le Saulchoir', concludes Guelluy.[22] Charlier was hardly known before the publication of his *Essai sur le problème théologique*; Chenu, on the other hand, had made himself many enemies thanks to his biting criticisms of several Roman theologians, and he proposed Le Saulchoir as a model for the formation of religious. His case was much more serious. The placing on the Index of *Une école de théologie* was therefore not purely collateral damage in the wake of the Charlier affair. Although his defence would be different, Chenu admitted at the time, 'What upsets me is that Le Saulchoir is under fire and attacked here, for they have not exhumed that little book for its own sake which has been buried for four years, since publication, to appease fraternal squabbles', he wrote to a religious friend on 4 April 1942.[23]

---

21. Quoted from the documentary file dated March 1942, which includes 'a note on the Charlier-Chenu friendship'; letters to Gilson dated 21 February 1942 or to the Franciscan Stéphane Piat dated 4 April. Gillet would return to this leitmotif for Congar in a letter dated 14 January 1946, Congar papers, ADF.
22. Guelluy, 'Les antécédents', p. 497.
23. Letter to Franciscan Stéphane Piat.

There was, then, a real debate between Chenu and his censors about the presentation of the Christian faith and the nature of the theology whose job was to give an account of it. Chenu continued to see his condemnation as an injustice based on a tissue of lies, and that immediate impression would be indelible, to the point that later he would refuse to look at the archived documents of the matter. 'I did not have the patience to re-read that text. What human misery. The poor church!', he noted in December 1977 for Fr Duval on an envelope which held a copy of a letter from Thomas Philippe to Garrigou-Lagrange dated 6-8 May 1942, rediscovered by the historian Andrea Riccardi in the archives of the Italian censor.[24]

2.3. Much Support, Some Criticisms

Published in a world torn apart by the war, the Holy Office decree hardly made the news: even in church circles, there were more pressing issues. Nonetheless, Chenu received a number of letters of support, beginning with those from his confreres in the French Dominican Province, and not only those he was closest to, like Congar, then a prisoner of war. 'I must say that the news from Ét[iolles] has played a part in a sort of depression I've had for the last 3 months, which I've now left behind, I think. It is hard to feel that one's home is being ravaged in one's absence, and to be powerless', he wrote to his friend Féret from Colditz on 14 September 1942. Later he would unceasingly seek to shed light on 'this improbable

---

24. Envelope containing a note from Congar to Duval, one from Duval to Chenu, Chenu's reply, and the photocopy of a document, ADF, probably December 1977.

matter.'[25] Unsurprisingly, Chenu received support from students at Le Saulchoir (Liégé), former pupils (Anawati, Gourbillon, Jomier, Louvel, Maydieu,[26] Régamey) and confreres (Noble, Réginald Omez, Vincent) for whom the matter was a real 'family bereavement'.[27] Sertillanges, who had plenty of experience of Roman sanctions, remained optimistic. 'You'll see, you'll see! After the rain comes the good weather. This is just an April shower. By saving the man we save everything, and we know who we have deal with', he wrote to Chenu on 26 March 1942. But Chenu also received more unexpected support. 'You know how I see things', wrote the very conservative Fr de Chivré to him, 'but I cannot be more sincere in the sympathy and prayer in which I hold you during these painful times for you'.[28] Given subsequent events, the most surprising of these letters came from Thomas Philippe. 'I pray wholeheartedly to the Holy Virgin that she herself may soften this harsh trial through those divine consolations to which she alone holds the secret', he wrote in his own Marian style.[29]

The Lyon Province was not excluded, as shown by a letter from Fr Lebret, founder of *Économie et Humanisme*, and another from Fr Bouëssé, professor at the Saint-Alban-Leysse *studium*, on the first anniversary of the sanction.[30] However, in Chenu's post at least, there was

---

25. Letter to Frs Avril and Féret dated 8 October 1942; see also his letters to Féret dated 14 December 1942 and 1 April 1943.
26. Passing on the support of Dubarle, a prisoner until October 1942, in a letter dated 11 June.
27. Interzone card from Fr Louvel, 27 [?] February.
28. Interzone card, 23 March (postmark).
29. Undated.
30. Interzone card dated 27 February 1942 and letter dated 3 March 1943.

nothing from the Toulouse Province. To know what they thought of the sanctioning of Chenu, we need to read the exchanges between Labourdette and his friend Nicolas. Far from rejoicing in a step which struck a competitor in Thomism, these two close friends of Maritain feared the worst for the consequences which it risked having on the whole of the Order in France. 'As you know, I of course do not like Fr Chenu's ideas or his tendencies; but this matter is playing out in a way that makes it very difficult to see what will follow with optimism', wrote Labourdette, while deploring the 'detestable species' of 'Chenu's supporters', 'with their combination of politeness, a vacuum, and pretentiousness'. The only good thing which could come out of the crisis, according to Labourdette, 'would be an *effective* reminder of the need to make every Dominican, or at least every Dominican who is to teach, undergo a serious study of the *Summa*, the whole *Summa*; and to precede that study with a truly Thomist, truly technical philosophy which is *learned*', without of course going through history.[31] A little later, when their confrere and friend Fr Lavaud, whom they were trying to get to return from the university of Fribourg, seemed under threat for his positions on marriage, the anxiety became more acute. 'This is a Terror, a new crisis like that of the time of Modernism, which risks opening up . . . We will probably have to work in silence for a long time—this is already the fate of the exegetes', wrote Labourdette at that point, or at least if they did not want 'to play the part of a Pègues or a Garrigou', or 'of a man who is still intelligent, like Fr Gagnebet', whose 'intrasigent and grand formulas . . . are not the most reassuring'.[32] Still as far removed as ever

---

31. Letter dated 27 February, confirmed in a letter dated 12 March, ADT.

32. Letter from Labourdette to Nicolas, 14 April 1942, ADT.

from Chenu's positions, the 'Toulousains' were not lining up alongside their Roman confreres as they had done in 1938, as they feared their rigour and narrow-mindedness.

Outwith the Order, the only unfavourable reaction, hardly surprisingly, came from the elderly Cardinal Baudrillart. 'Despite the vigorous opposition of the Italian and Spanish Dominicans, who have seen things as they are', the '*democratic* utopias of our French ignoramuses' have continued on their way, at the risk of a schism or a return to integrism, he wrote in his diary on 6 March 1942. Yet on 11 March, it was nothing more than 'a sinister *joke* from the Council of vigilantes which has been re-established now', to which he promised to submit the following questions: 'M. D. Chenu. Père Congar? Étiolles. Rue de la Glacière. Université catholique, doctrine du Saulchoir'.[33] Was there a discussion of the matter during this meeting? And if yes, what was the result? A week before it took place, the St Sulpician, Fr Louis Augros, alerted Chenu that the Archbishop of Paris, Cardinal Suhard, would have refused to mention the sanction in his *Semaine religieuse* 'had he not been asked to do so from on high'.[34] Suhard had received the file on the matter from the Holy Office which Garrigou-Lagrange was to summarise for him in person.[35] Chenu's papers only include a single reaction from a bishop: a minimal note from the auxilliary bishop of Versailles, Mgr Henri Audrain, who mentioned obedience, sacrifice, and redemptive suffering.[36] Mgr Beaussart, Auxilliary Bishop of Paris, was said to be 'furious', but there is no

---

33. *Les Carnets du cardinal Baudrillart*, 369–371.

34. Letter dated 5 March 1942.

35. Letter from Cardinal Marchetti-Selvaggiani dated 23 February, Archives historiques de l'archevêché de Paris, 2 A II 3.

36. Letter dated 12 March.

written trace of his anger.[37] Mgr Bruno de Solages, Rector of the Institut catholique de Toulouse, on the other hand, who was 'absolutely furious' about the episode,[38] was not content to reassure his friend of his 'fraternal and sorrowful sympathy',[39] but also appealed to another friend in Rome, Cardinal Eugène Tisserant. 'Anyone who is anyone in the theological world has been sadly touched by what has happened to Fr Chenu, and the consequences worry me greatly. Is there nothing we can do to prevent them opening fire on our best troops, particularly at a time when communications prevent us from intervening, explaining, and defending?', he wrote to Tisserant on 28 July 1942.[40] But Tisserant, Secretary to the Congregation for Oriental Churches, was not a member of the Holy Office, and therefore had no say on doctrinal questions. On 27 July, Chenu decided to write to Suhard. 'Please believe, dear Father, that I am not indifferent to your trial, and that my most fervent wish is to bring you comfort in the suffering you are enduring', replied Suhard on 30 July, before offering a meeting on 3 August which would be delayed until the end of that month. Was it during this meeting that Suhard quipped what Chenu later claimed: 'Dear Father, do not worry, in twenty years everyone will be talking as you do'.[41] There is no trace of this in Suhard's papers, nor in his journal, any more than there is of the explicit request from Chenu, dated 2 January 1943,

---

37. Letter from Chenu to Étienne Gilson dated 7 March.
38. According to Fr Prétaudoux, letter from Labourdette to Nicolas dated 12 March, ADT.
39. Letter dated 1 March.
40. Letter published in the *Bulletin de littérature ecclésiastique* (January –June 1998): 126.
41. *Un théologien en liberté*, 121; similar words in *Hommage différé*, 267.

that Suhard intervene on his behalf in Rome during his upcoming *ad limina* visit.[42] According to Motte, 'in Rome Cardinal Suhard was given two documents addressed to us, which he did not want to take responsibility for: a letter from Father General on studies, and another letter notifying us of the conclusions of the apostolic visitation on behalf of the Holy Office.'[43] Hence the disappointment shared by someone close to the Cardinal, Bouëssé: 'What you have entrusted to me from Emmanuel [Suhard] upsets me but does not surprise me . . . I have learned how timid, to say the least, those who should show themselves to be leaders can be. They express their judgement which agrees totally with ours . . . and do nothing', he wrote to Chenu on 1 May 1943. We can therefore hardly say that Chenu 'received numerous letters of sympathy from the French episcopate', as Draguet, himself under threat, wrote.[44]

In the absence of support from the hierarchy there was no lack of compassion from his theological friends for Chenu, now dismissed as Rector of Le Saulchoir. From Fourvière, the Jesuit, Henri de Lubac, Fr Jean Mouroux, from the major seminary in Dijon, and the Oratorian Gaston Rabeau, well known to readers of the *Revue des sciences philosophiques et théologiques*, not to mention the German theologian, Friedrich Stegmüller, author of one of the few reviews of *Une école de théologie*, all sent

---

42. Draft in Chenu's papers.

43. Letter quoted by Thomas Deman to Chenu, 9 February 1943; there is nothing further on this matter in the Cardinal's journal.

44. Letter to his pupil, the Servite Vincenzo Buffon, 27 May 1942 (translated by the Italian censor, rediscovered by Andrea Riccardi who quotes it in *Roma, "città sacra"?* (Milan: Vita e pensiero, 1979), 235.

their sympathy and solidarity in his '"captivity" which is sadly liberating', as Mouroux put it, in the words of the time. For his part Daniélou wrote that 'the Chenu affair is odious'. In his account of the inaugural lecture of the chair of history of spirituality at the Institut catholique de Paris on 15 November 1943, Daniélou drew Étienne Gilson in the direction for which Chenu was blamed. 'While M. Gilson has not spoken about this, the whole of his work is evidence to show us that a major theology corresponded to every major spirituality, and that St Augustine, St Bernard, St Thomas, and St Bonaventure each had a theology for their spirituality'.[45] In 1942, Chenu was no longer known solely by theologians, but also by the apostles of the home mission, to whom he became one of the most listened-to counsellors, hence his presence among the supporters of Fr Dominique Mesnard, chaplain to the Jeunesse Maritime Chrétienne and his confrere in the la Jeunesse Ouvrière, Fr Albert Bouche, who admitted how much they owed him.[46] Above all there was Augros, rector of the seminary of the Mission de France then was starting out at Lisieux, to whom Chenu was a much-valued guide,[47] or Fr Jean Rodhain, national chaplain to prisoners of war.[48]

---

45. Letter dated 5 March to Fr de Lubac, in *Bulletin des amis du cardinal Daniélou*, 2 (June 1976): 64; and in *Revue du Moyen Âge latin* 1 (1945): 65.
46. Letters dated 26 February and 3 March.
47. 'Do tell him that he has *all* my trust, and that I continue to count on him in the same way to help us', he wrote to Fr Épagneul, founder of the Frères missionnaires des campagnes, on 17 April (letter copied by Chenu). In his letter of support dated 5 March, he sent Chenu the booklet introducing the Mission de France.
48. Undated.

From lay intellectuals, Fr Chenu's notoriety sufficed to raise a salvo of condolences. The very Gallican Louis Canet, counsellor for religious affairs at the French Foreign Office, twice demonstrated his compassionate sympathy. It must be said that, like the unedited precedents by Fr Laberthonnière which he published, the *Études de philosophie cartésienne et premiers écrits philosophiques* were victims of the Index on 29 March 1941.[49] The draft of a response kept by Chenu proves that his later successor, law professor Gabriel Le Bras, offered to intervene on his behalf with Gillet.[50] The author Daniel-Rops and the philosopher Henri Gouhier also came out in his support,[51] although there was nothing from Jacques Maritain, then in exile in the United States, and who was particularly concerned about the fate of Fr Lavaud, but nonetheless thought about the affair. 'Chenu dismissed from Le Saulchoir and his programme placed on the Index. Garrigou trimphant.' 'I fear that Pastor Angelicus is a divine irony, and how cruel', he wrote to his disciple Yves Simon about 'poor Chenu'.[52] But Chenu's main confidant immediately following the sanction was none other than Étienne Gilson with whom he had worked closely for nearly twenty years. 'The news which

---

49. Paris, Librairie philosophique Vrin, 1937. Interzone cards dated 8 and 29 April.

50. Undated draft in pencil.

51. Sent on 15 March and 3 June.

52. *Correspondance Jacques Maritain-Yves Simon*, volume 2, Les années américaines (1941–1961) (edition established and annotated by Florian Michel (Tours: CLD éditions, 2012), 100–101 (letters of 27 and 29 May 1942); letter to Fr Charles Journet dated 25 July. Pastor angelicus was the title given to Pius XII by the late-sixteenth-century prophecy attributed to St Malachy.

you have sent would just have made me laugh, did I not know how much terrible pain being placed on the Index must have caused you', Gilson replied to him on 27 February, for it seemed so improbable. He assessed the weight of suffering for the victim and the repercussions for intellectual work in the church, while hoping that the blow would not interrupt his friend's 'work as a Master of Sacred Theology'. Having re-read *Une école de théologie*, he continued, far from doing Thomism a disservice, the condemned booklet sought to return it 'to a concrete plan'. Like Motte, he felt that Chenu's sin was to have criticised speculative Thomists, and they had taken their revenge. It was necessary to continue to work in the same vein, but 'thinking more of the human weaknesses which one has to manage so that their revolt does not turn against truth itself'.[53] Deeply troubled by this 'lamentable story' both as a historian of medieval philosophy and as a Christian, Gilson proposed helping Chenu, now forbidden to teach, to obtain a research bursary at the newly founded Centre National de la Recherche Scientifique.[54]

3. The Apostolic Visitation

The visitation of the Belgian Dominican house of studies at La Sarte, near Huy, was entrusted to Fr Matthijs, who had been one of the examiners of *Une école de théologie* in Rome in 1938. According to Robert Guelluy, the visitation was very courteous, although it still led to Charlier's retirement from teaching and the appointment of Fr Matthijs as the Regent of Studies.[55] For the three French

---

53. Letter dated 28 February 1942, in *Revue thomiste*, 105 (2005): 52–53.

54. Letter dated 8 June, in *Revue thomiste*, 105 (2005) 56-57.

55. Guelluy, 'Les antécédents', 487.

Dominican houses of study and their publishing houses, the Holy Office appointed Garrigou-Lagrange as apostolic visitor in a letter of 27 February 1942. Although Gillet himself cleared Garrigou-Lagrange of any immediate responsibility for the sanctions against Chenu, his arrival still caused anxiety, and not only at Le Saulchoir. While Labourdette was happy that a Dominican was sent to the French Province, he thought Garrigou 'is the last one who should have been given this work', for he feared that Garrigou would become 'the führer of the French Dominican theologians',[56] although Saint-Maximin had nothing to worry about. 'Fr Garrigiou's visitation passed without drama', he wrote to his friend Nicolas on 15 June 1942, although it must be said that the Visitor began by saying, 'I know that there is nothing to deal with *here*'.[57] Neither did his visitation of the Lyon *studium* cause any waves.

3.1. Garrigou-Lagrange

The same could not be said for Le Saulchoir, in preparation for which Garrigou-Lagrange had prepared detailed documents.[58] Tasked by the Holy Office with 'seeing if the errors contained in the two books which have been condemned are more or less accepted by some minds to the detriment of the intellectual formation

---

56. Letter to Nicolas, 27 February, ADT.

57. According to the delayed reverberation received on 16 September 1954 by Fr Congar, typed note, Congar papers.

58. 'Lettre annonçant la visite canonique', copy made at the Angelicum on Fr Garrigou-Lagranges hand-written notes, by Fr Paul Coutagne, of the Lyon Province, 7 typed pages; handwritten document of 14 pages in Fr Thomas Philippe's file for the visitation, ADF.

which must be offered in our houses of study', he was
aware of the delicate nature of his task, 'given that one
of the two condemned books was written by a former
pupil of mine, who teaches in my province'. In order
to discuss the 'deviations' the two works contained, he
would begin by reading the commentary of the decree
published 'in *Osservatore Romano* by a Consultor to the
Holy Office at the request of the Holy Office itself', then
emphasising 'the main points which the deviations under
discussion are about.' According to Garrigou, these were
five. 1) An erroneous judgment about the seriousness
of the Modernist crisis, wrongly presented as simply a
crisis of growth in a healthy body (referring to page 38
of *Une école de théologie*). 2) The 'bringing into disrepute
of scholastic philosophy and theology' which the Roman
pontiffs since Leo XIII had advocated. While the Visitor
regretted Chenu's critiques of 'baroque scholasticism'
(*Une école de théologie*, page 85) and picked up on his
formula according to which 'there is no worse disgrace
for Thomism than to be treated as "orthodoxy" (*Une
école de théologie*, page 76), his main charge was against
Draguet, who would be removed from his post in July
1942 without formal condemnation, and his disciple,
Charlier.[59] 3) The 'depreciation of proofs *ex S. Scripturae
et ex Traditione* which are commonly accepted': here
Garrigou-Lagrange was contesting Chenu's preface to the
second edition of Ambroise Gardeil's *Donné révélé et la
théologie*, before again attacking Draguet and Charlier,
along with their supposed inspiration, the Tübingen
theologian, Johann Adam Möhler. If these proofs were
brought into disrepute, 'we would be on the way to a
semi-Modernism'. 4) There was 'an internal growth of the

---

59. Guelluy, 'Les antécédents', 472–478; also in particular see
Ward De Pril's book.

deposit of Revelation', which according to Möhler—the only one mentioned here—was therefore not closed. 5) Finally, Garrigou-Lagrange regretted the substitution of religious experience for the church's magisterium, which led directly to relativism, and he picked up Chenu's now-famous expression: 'a theology worthy of its name is a spirituality which has found rational tools appropriate to its religious experience (*Une école de théologie*, page 75). As we can see the charge is serious and, in addition to Parente's complaints, included a number of Garrigou-Lagrange's own pet hates, such as Blondel's definition of the truth, which was itself quite foreign to the accused Dominicans. Far from restricting himself to the sanctioned works, from which he cited few passages, the Visitor trained the process into a fictitious lineage going from Möhler and Blondel to Draguet, and from Draguet to Charlier and to Chenu. Chenu challenged this lineage for its relevance: while he admitted his debt to Möhler and the Tübingen school, he denied any influence from Draguet or Charlier on his own thought.

At the end of his indictment, Garrigou-Lagrange reckoned that he would need only three days for the visitation during which he would interrogate all the superiors, professors and students at Le Saulchoir on these questions, while imposing the apostolic secret on them.

3.2. Thomas Philippe

Despite his plans, Garrigou-Lagrange did not go to Le Saulchoir, where he was expected to arrive on 17 or 18 March 1942,[60] but his summing up lost nothing for this. On

---

60. Dates given by Motte when he arrived at Le Saulchoir (house chronicle).

24 April, he announced to Motte that he had been unable to obtain the 'passport "visa"' for the occupied zone in which Le Saulchoir, now at Étiolles, had found itself since 1939. According to Marie-Dominique Philippe, this was merely a pretext, as Garrigou-Lagrange would have been 'absolutely scared stiff of going to Le Saulchoir', guessing that he would not be welcome there. He therefore begged Thomas Philippe, who had been detained in Paris since 1940, to replace him.[61] Whatever the case, Gillet, who wrote positively about Thomas Philippe in his journal,[62] passed on to Motte the very next day, the Holy Office's appointment of Philippe as apostolic visitor and Regent of Studies *ad interim*. Philippe's letter to Garrigou-Lagrange dated 6–8 May, intercepted by the Italian censor, proves that he was indeed the 'sub-delegate'.[63] 'It was your letter dated 23 April which brought me the news of the position entrusted to me', he wrote, having received nothing at that stage from either the Holy Office or the General Curia. While there are very diverse opinions on the roots of the affair, the witnesses all agree about Philippe's unsuitability for the mission which fell to him. Born in 1905, he was only third-seven years of age, which was very young for such a role. He had entered the French Province in 1923, and completed all his studies at Le Saulchoir, teaching there

---

61. *Les trois sagesses* (Paris: Fayard, 1995), 220–221.
62. 'Permission refused for Fr Garrigou. What are we to do? Appointment of Fr Père Thomas Philippe, rector and Visitor. Former professor at the Angelicum, a very reliable and holy religious. His only fault is that he is still young', journal entry dated 12 April 1942, quoted by Dominique Avon in *Les Frères prêcheurs en Orient. Les dominicains du Caire* (années 1920-années 1960) (Paris: Cerf, 2005), 347.
63. Le Saulchoir house chronical dated 5 May, edited by Fr André Duval.

until his transfer to the Angelicum in 1936. A pupil and then a co-worker of Chenu's, he was poorly placed to put the decisions taken against him into effect. From a large, middle-class family in the Nord département, he was also the nephew and spiritual son of Fr Thomas Dehau, and had three brothers in the province, one of whom, Marie-Dominique, was teaching at Le Saulchoir in 1942. Today this would be raised as a risk of a conflict of interest.[64] Finally, and this is more difficult to discern with justice and fairness, he was temperamentally unsuitable. Chenu, a sure judge and jury, wrote to Suhard that 'his youth, his inexperience, his lack of culture, and his lack of spiritual freedom' hardly qualified him for such a task.[65] With more hindsight we can say that he lacked reasoned, or critical, mediation between his speculative intellectualism and his unbridled Marian piety, fed by a private revelation in a church in Rome in 1938. Even his brother felt that his appointment had led to a series of 'gaffes'.[66] For his part, Desroches noted that his 'slenderness turned out to be fragility'.[67]

While Motte offered in vain to come to Rome and carry out the canonical visitation of Le Saulchoir as though it were nothing, Thomas Philippe was preparing himself for his work by entrusting 'the whole affair to the Most Holy Virgin, Sedes Sapientiae, that She may give me light and strength and that I may be Her good, docile, flexible instrument', as he wrote to Garrigou-Lagrange on 6 May. 'This was all entrusted to me at the start of her month, and I shall take it as her servant who puts all his trust in

---

64. In addition to Marie-Dominique, Pierre and Réginald Philippe (who died of illness in 1940).
65. Draft of a letter dated 2 January 1943.
66. Marie-Dominique Philippe, page 221.
67. 'Avec Chenu mémorial d'un magistère', page 4.

Her.' He was relying on the advice of his mentor, whose authorised representative he seemed to be. Three times he clarified that he would fulfil his task with discretion and with firmness.[68] Installed as Regent of Studies on 7 or 8 May by Motte,[69] he could however not begin his visitation as planned, because Garrigou-Lagrange's letter of 23 April did not have the semi-official nature he believed it did. On the advice of Suhard, he went to the free zone to be able to correspond more easily with Rome.[70] We can easily imagine the trouble such a hitch gave rise to at Le Saulchoir, while awaiting the ordeal. Fr Avril, the Prior who had returned from imprisonment, twice offered his resignation, and then requested that he be removed if the suspicion of him were linked to his praise of Chenu's booklet, now on the Index.[71]

Finally, on 6 June 1942, the visitation could begin. The provincial read the document from the Secretary of the Holy Office dated 27 February, naming Garrigou-Lagrange as apostolic visitor of the Order's three colleges and the Dominican publishing houses in France, and then the document dated 25 April appointing Thomas Philippe as his replacement in the occupied zone and provisional Regent of Le Saulchoir, and finally the document from Garrigou-Lagrange handing over his authority to Philippe. Philippe then explained 'that he had seen Fr Garrigou-Lagrange at length in the free zone and had

---

68. Letter quoted dated 6–8 May 1942.

69. According to his undated letter to Gillet, this was on 7 May, AGOP XIII 30200/2 file 12; according to the Le Saulchoir chronicle it was 8 May.

70. Letter to Gillet, undated (14 May on the document), AGOP XIII 30200/2 file 12.

71. Correspondence with Motte between 15 May and 12 June, ADF.

been able to familiarise himself with a whole file dealing with the condemnation of a book by Fr Chenu'.[72] He had come to explain the reasons for this sanction and to draw up a report 'which Fr Garrigou-Lagrange would complete and send on to the Holy Office'. He was nothing more than Garrigou's shadow! Having read Parente's article, which was 'written for the faithful, not for theologians, hence some simplifications and indecisiveness',[73] he summarised for the whole college, and then for the lectors alone, the complaints about the two books in five points, those of the documents prepared by Garrigou. Fr Dewailly wrote that,

> There followed a very discreet exchange of opinions. In particular, Fr Chenu indicated some confusions in the preliminary investigations of the matter. Several lacunae in the visitor's documentation came to light (no knowledge of Congar's revivew of Gagnebet and Charlier, or the propositions Fr Chenu had signed in 38; Fr Motte reflected that 'the business in 37 was all for nothing'). Fr Héris asked on what exact points not only Fr Chenu but the whole of Le Saulchoir was under suspicion, evasive reply. Plan for a draft or propositions which the professors would sign.[74]

Such a text would of course have been drawn up by Héris and signed by all the professors, including Chenu. Thomas Philippe's lectures to students on 2, 9, and 27 June reprised each of these points in detail, following Garrigou-Lagrange's preparatory text to the letter—the

---

72. His file for the visitation included a 14-page document in Garrigou-Lagrange's writing, ADF.

73. 'Notes taken day to day during the successive meetings with the college lectors', Louis-Marie Dewailly.

74. Same source.

same complaints backed up by the same passages from *d'Une école de théologie*.[75] Thomas Philippe's dependence on his mentor was such that we might talk about Fr Garrigou-Lagrange's visitation by proxy. In the meantime, the Visitor individually interrogated, under formal rules, each of the religious assigned to Le Saulchoir, both students and professors.

Various clues found in the correspondence between the Provincial and the General Curia as well as in Chenu's papers, hint that the visitation went less well than Thomas Philippe reported to Rome, in that it raised ill-feeling among both the young lectors and the students. 'I feel that there is quite a heavy atmosphere at Le Saulchoir', Motte wrote to Louis on 20 June. 'Rightly or wrongly, I don't know which, we are fearful of a real cleansing, which makes us apprehensive about the future.' Was it only Chenu and his methodology which were the targets, or Le Saulchoir as a whole, where very different opinions on this methodology co-existed more or less happily? Personally subdued, Chenu could only resign himself to seeing 'Le Saulchoir, its mind-set, its works, its curiosity, its conquest, the Le Saulchoir of Gardeil, Lemonnyer, Mandonnet, questioned; under threat, already condemned in a plan to allow him to maintain his powers and faculties, but emptied of all substance'.[76] The encumbrance was not completely lifted until the end of June when the visitation was completed, in the material sense of the term, although not canonically.[77] Thomas Philippe's visitation to the house of St Dominic, home of les Éditions du Cerf, on the boulevard Latour-Maubourg, has left hardly any traces. According to Chenu it was

---

75. Notes from Duval on his lessons, typed, 5 pages and 2 pages.
76. Letter to Duval, 11 July.
77. Letter from Motte to Louis, 27 June, ADF, copy.

'amicably basic' and 'concluded without complaints'.[78] Such serenity was not shared by his provincial. 'I do not really understand how this matter has been judged, and yet the measures which are announced are so serious that they suppose serious wrongs and errors', he wrote on 28 September. 'Fr Visitor has left nothing to give rise to such suspicion, and in fact, since the war I have heard no complaints about the house's publications, aside from the inadequate place given to the Encyclicals in the "*Spiritualité de la famille*", which is hardly the same as a doctrinal error'.[79]

3.3. The fate of *Revue des sciences philosophiques et théologiques*

Thomas Philippe completed his report during the summer of 1942,[80] and Paul Philippe passed it on to the Holy Office. 'He told me', wrote Labourdette to his friend Nicolas, 'that this report was . . . "absolutely admirable", running through every synonym in the French language for "admirable" to try to describe this landmark document, which also sent Fr Garrigou into raptures. Fr Paul is purely and simply happy with the condemnation (in the field of ideas), and he thinks this clears the air'.[81] However, much to the annoyance of the provincial and the prior, who wanted a return to a normal situation, if not to normality, as soon as possible, not to mention the

---

78. Draft of a letter to Mgr Beaussart, 27 October.

79. Letter to Louis, copy in ADF. *Spiritualité de la famille* was the 8th volume of the 'Rencontres' series founded at Cerf by Fr Maydieu the previous year; it was published in 1942.

80. His file for the visitation includes a 45-page handwritten draft, ADF.

81. Letter dated 22 August 1942, ADT.

possible victims, they had to wait for the results of the visitation. This was even more the case since the visitor increased initiatives which seemed to them to go beyond his initial mandate. 'University professors, such as Gilson, cannot inform us on particular points: they must not become our masters', he stated in his lesson opening the 1942–1943 university year, despite himself claiming to be a follower of Jacques Maritain.[82] Above all he attacked the *Revue des sciences philosophiques et théologiques* which had until then escaped his attention,[83] as its publication had been put on hold since 1940. 'But when we saw that an issue which we had not initially planned could be published, we felt obliged to notify him', explained Louis.[84] The fact remains that Thomas Philippe wrote to Garrigou-Lagrange in December 1942 to ask him what would be appropriate to do about the journal. 'As I had imagined, Fr Garrigou told me it seemed impossible that Fr Chenu remain as editor, and he suggested replacing him with Fr Guérard des Lauriers', he wrote in a letter whose recipient found it 'very formal' and thus binding.[85] On 24 January, he only found the strength to inform Chenu of his removal from the journal to which he had given so much 'from his Crucifix'. Almost certainly Guérard, promoted to 'editorial secretary for the duration' in place of Congar, then a prisoner of war, which was to say the least particularly clumsy, 'did not have the social qualities of a journal editor: he was purely academic, loving his ivory tower almost excessively', but he was not suspected

---

82. According to Le Saulchoir house chronicle.

83. 'Neither did he read the final volumes' of the journal, Chenu confirmed in the note which he inserted into the second edition of *La théologie comme science au XIIIe siècle*.

84. Letter to Motte, 2 May 1943.

85. Letter to Gillet, 13 February, AGOP XIII 30200/2 file 12.

of excessive sympathy for Chenu's ideas.[86] Entitled *Les sciences religieuses*, an issue dated 1941–1942 was in fact published, in which Guérard gave himself the lion's share, with two philosophical articles on induction. The late inclusion of Chenu's symbolic mouthpiece in the Visitor's mandate confirmed that it was indeed not him alone, but the whole of Le Saulchoir, in the Roman firing line.

Although his personal setbacks had only caused the former Regent to demonstrate exemplary obedience, this new blow gave him a new zeal for war. In his view, by changing the editorial board of the *Revue des sciences philosophiques et théologiques*, Thomas Philippe went beyond his authority. And thus the cup overflowed: on 2 February 1943, Chenu expressed his reservations about a measure which he would accept at a personal level but which he rejected to the extent that it 'affected the structure' of the journal and risked changing its direction. 'A journal is a soul, a foundation of trust and mind-set, not a post office', he argued.[87] His appeal for support in order that the work undertaken could continue to make progress was sufficiently widespread to worry the provincial.[88] When on 4 February Thomas Philippe presented his decision to the termly council of lectors, the rebellion became open. 'Historic meeting last night', wrote Deman to Chenu. 'The visitor defeated once and for all. No one intervened on his behalf. He stammered pathetic responses . . . the R. S.

---

86. Born in 1898, Michel (Louis-Bertrand in religion) Guérard des Lauriers entered the École normale supérieure in 1921, being awarded a degree in Mathematics in 1924 and a
   · doctorate in sciences in 1941. As a Dominican of the French Province from 1926 he taught epistemology and philosophy of science at Le Saulchoir.

87. Draft in Chenu's papers.

88. Letter to Chenu dated 4 February.

P. T. was defended as it should have been.'[89] Less lyrically, Duval noted the reservations of the elderly Fr Allo, who had retired to le Saulchoir, on the clumsy way in which Chenu had been thrown out; Deman's reservations on its legitimacy because the decision had been taken without waiting for the conclusions of the visitation and 'without consultation of the journal's editorial board'; and those of Fr Féret 'about the tendentious side of this removal'. Thomas Philippe himself agreed that he had brought about 'violent reactions', and some lectors, 'considering the measure to be arbitrary, questioned my authority to make this decision, and that of Fr Garrigou'. He had to close the meeting hurriedly 'as Visitor, I could not tolerate these dressing-downs'.[90] It was as though the matter had been the straw that broke the camel's back. As long as the visitation had remained within the bounds which had been initially anticipated, Chenu and his personal guard of young lectors could only bow their heads and submit. But as soon as it seemed to them that Thomas Philippe had gone beyond his authority, they took advantage of the situation to express their undisguised unhappiness his visitation had created at Le Saulchoir.

What is more things did not stop here. As requested by Chenu, 'M. Vrin, in complete agreement with M. Gilson, his publishing adviser, has decided to stop publishing the *Revue*'. For them, the journal was not only 'a quarterly collection of articles and reviews', but 'an expression of a mind-set, a methodology, a friendship', as Chenu explained to the editorial board, asking them to forward the information to those who worked with them, but not to Thomas Philippe, who learned about

---

89. Letter incorrectly dated 5 February 1942, which led Dominique Avon astray (*Les Frères prêcheurs en Orient,* 347).
90. Letter to Gillet, AGOP XIII 30200/2 file 12.

it from Guérard des Lauriers.[91] 'In university circles just as in ecclesial circles, both in France and abroad, the *Revue* gained huge credibility through its mind-set and its academic probity.' Since the predicted bringing to heel could no longer guarantee this mind-set, the publisher, who had made financial sacrifices to maintain it, could no longer carry on. From an intellectual perspective 'it is better that we don't add any ambiguity . . . to those which already surround us and that the same flag is not used to cover other things', Chenu continued, justifying Vrin's decision, although it had agreed to Henri Gouhier's requests in particular to start publishing again, following the break since 1940. Le Saulchoir would lose the material benefit of eighty journals in exchange and 40,000 francs of books in review and, above all, the spiritual benefit of 'an active and acute presence among the problems and the religious work of our contemporaries'.[92] Chenu received Deman's approval, as he had taken the initiative in sending his letter to a meeting of those who worked with the journal and had had a serious altercation with Thomas Philippe, whom he held entirely responsible for Vrin's decision;[93] he also had the approval of Héris and Congar. 'I approve of the suspension of the R[evue] Sciences. This is a q[uestion] of honour', Congar wrote to Féret from Colditz on 1 April. Even Motte, who had to beat a retreat before Chenu's ire, kept his distance from the Visitor: the decisions taken about the *Revue des sciences* 'were not urgent' and 'were poorly carried out, giving the impression of a rather underhand overthrow', he wrote to Louis on 27 February.

---

91. Lettre to Chenu dated 15 February.

92. Letter to the editorial board, dated 11 February, copy.

93. Lengthy letter to Chenu dated 17 February.

After many delays due to the slow post in occupied
France, the conclusions of the visitation eventually arrived
in Paris and at Le Saulchoir. The letter Cardinal Marchetti-
Selvaggiani, Secretary to the Holy Office, sent to Gillet,
who was tasked with applying them, is dated 3 November
1942.[94] Gillet's repeated dispatches diverge on points of
detail, which does not facilitate their interpretation.[95] On
26 March 1943, having received a letter from Gillet dated
26 February, Thomas Philippe called a meeting first of
the lectors of Le Saulchoir, and then of the students, to
draw the visitation to a close. Reporting on his mission
to the Master General, he opposed the good spirits of the
students with the bad spirit remaining among the lectors.
'I sense a silent opposition among some of them, which
is not waning'.[96] Several lectors—Tonneau, Féret, and
Dubarle, according to a note from Dewailly—demanded
'official papers, directly from the Holy Office, for the
installation of a new governing body' and the canonical
conclusion of the visitation.[97] Gillet had to clarify that
'there are no other documents apart from the letter which
deals with the decisions of the visitation, for according

---

94. Copy in the Archives historiques de l'archevêché de Paris, 2
    A II/3.
95. An initial letter from Gillet to Motte dated 10 December
    1942 only arrived in Paris on 4 April 1943. 'I am sending the
    conclusions of the visitation for the fourth time', Gillet wrote
    on 7 March; this letter was received on 24 April according to
    the Provincial's reply dated 26 April, ADF.
96. Letter dated 30 March, AGOP XIII 30200/2 file 12.
97. Note dated 26 March. 'Very Rev Fr. Philippe informs us that
    the Visitation [. . .] has not ended, as the official documents
    have not yet arrived. Fr Visitor read us a passage from a
    letter from Most Rev Fr General, letting us know the main
    decisions of the Holy Office', the house chronicle records for
    the same date.

to the rules of the Holy Office it is Fr General alone who is informed of the decisions and who applies them'. Very firmly, he invited the provincial to 'first of all be himself convinced', and 'then to convince his subordinates' of the vanity of the 'commentaries', 'suspicion' and 'hypotheses' about the sanctions to which they had to submit without discussion or 'recrimination'.[98] The visitation thus came to an end on 7 May 1943. Thomas Philippe was promoted to Master of Sacred Theology on 11 May, his letters patent having been sent by Gillet to Motte on 7 March. Thus 'after 15 long months of uncertainty', a trial which had left all the protagonists 'on edge' came to an end.[99]

4. Serious Consequences

4.1. Gillet's Encyclical Letter

Although this lineage was not admitted, the crisis gave rise to Gillet's lengthy encyclical—103 printed pages, with French at the top, Latin at the bottom—on 'the teaching of St Thomas at the present moment'. Dated 13 November 1942, the feast of St Thomas, it made no mention of the matter, but its author himself viewed it as part of the fallout. 'I wrote it, not for my own pleasure, but out of a duty of conscience before the ease with which in certain Provinces . . . doctrinal positions of major importance in philosophy and theology have been abandoned', he wrote to Motte on 7 March 1943. 'It behoves provincials to keep a close eye on these movements, and I regret to say that all too often they have encouraged them, there is no doubt of this.' As an example, he mentioned the books by Charlier and Chenu approved by censors including two former

---

98. Letter to Motte, which arrived on 6 May, ADF.
99. Lettre from Motte to Gillet, 11 June, ADF, copy.

provincials.[100] The encyclical, which does not seem to have been sent out earlier than mid-March,[101] was to be read in every house and in the *studia* once a year on 13 November. From the introduction the Master General took a position on one of the then controversial questions. 'Here and there', he wrote, 'we have noted such defiance towards reason and the traditional truths to the benefit of what has been vaguely termed "modern ideas" that the very idea of the truth remains falsified. Rather than seeing it following the understanding of the wisdom of antiquity, the conformity of understanding with reality— *adaequatio rei et intellectus*—which leads to objective judgements, it has been claimed that one can add to its definition new and subjective elements such as feeling, action, and life.'[102] Here Gillet was judging an old quarrel between Thomists in general, and Garrigou-Lagrange in particular, against the thought of Maurice Blondel and its supposed infiltrations into the Order. The first part of the encyclical, on 'the teaching of St Thomas in philosophy', warned young religious against the temptations of modern philosophy, knowledge of which should only come in third place in their formation after a personal and in-depth study of St Thomas, alongside the great commentators, all in Latin, for the meaning of the Latin words 'remains fixed for ever', unlike the changing vocabulary of modern languages and therefore philosophies.[103] Far from 'lazy conservatism', a conservatism 'in the highest and noblest

---

100. Letter erroneously dated 7 October 1943, received 24 April.

101. The first Roman and French acknowledgements of receipt in the file kept by Gillet are those dated 13 March and 2 April, AGOP V 306.

102. Page 6; very similar formula in the body of the text, pages 47–48.

103. Page 28.

meaning of this word' should govern the teaching of
Thomist philosophy,[104] which is *the* Christian philosophy,
the only one capable of harmonising reason and faith for
an objective apprehension of the Being and beings.

The second part of the encyclical, on 'the teaching of
St Thomas' doctrine in theology', while affirming the need
for a comparison with modern intellectual disciplines,
noted that this was responsible for a malaise among
theologians, and the imprudence of some of them.

> While they do not yet call this subject new
> theology, they do at least allow themselves to speak
> about a new direction in theology. And it is in this
> name that they bitterly complain about backward
> theologians stuck in the past, enclosed in their
> theological system as though in an ivory tower
> . . . endlessly spinning around in their syllogisms
> . . . ignoring through their prejudice the progress
> of history and criticism, that is, clinging on to
> scholastic formulas as though to a lifebuoy.

The allusion to the crisis then happening is even clearer
given that Gillet repeats the formula 'new theology'
which had appeared in Parente's commentary on the
decree in February. Excessive complaints, he commented,
while once more rejecting the 'lazy conservatism' of
professors who were 'more attached to the letter than
the spirit of St Thomas.[105] Of course it was necessary to
cultivate positive theology, but 'it is not enough to be a
good historian to be a good theologian. Theology needs
history, but history is not sufficient . . . . to establish all
the revealed truths which are the starting point for

---

104. Pages 32–33.
105. Pages 52–53.

speculative theology.[106] Gillet's preference was thus for speculative theology, through which 'reason proves what faith approves',[107] and he emphasised the decisive role of analogy in its deductive methodology. No one would have carried out this programme better than St Thomas, with his great knowledge of the Bible, the Fathers, and the academic disciplines of his times, as well as being a master of metaphysics. Yet his example had not extinguished the trials between the 'positives' and the 'speculatives': while the former were not wrong to complain that the latter 'neglected the academic study of the sources of the faith, the "speculatives" were entirely right to complain of the current tendencies of certain "positives", whose principal, and in our opinion most dangerous, tendency, is their lack of appreciation or the impression they give of not appreciating the use of reason itself in theology, in the name of the abuse made of this by some theologians'.[108] Was this the judgement of Solomon putting the protagonists back to back? Not really, for Gillet maintained the Thomist ideal of a rational philosophy integrated into theology as the best approach to Christian faith, and took a clear position against appeal to religious experience, which imperilled the nature of theology, even if that were not its aim, and 'fatally, more or less camouflaged, introduced the doctrine of the development of dogma'.[109] The criticisms against the conservatism of some of his adversaries were unable to disguise the condemnation of certain positions attributed to the sanctioned religious, particularly Chenu. The practical conclusions were in the same direction, since they gave the Order's Roman

---

106. Page 58.
107. Page 65.
108. Page 76.
109. Pages 85–86.

college a right to inspect the quality of Thomism taught in the *studia* of the provinces: Gillet planned to bring the regents of study and professors together at the Angelicum every three years. The formation of students could only take place in the *studia*, where lessons in scholastic theology and philosophy had to be in Latin. Finally, the checking of journals needed to be more rigorous: 'no religious, priest, or lay-person, whose ultra-modern or anti-Thomist tendencies are notorious, may be allowed to work alongside us on the Journals'.[110]

As if reading the encyclical were not enough, Motte's acknowledgement of receipt confirmed that this calling to order of the Dominicans was indeed the intellectual consequence of the trial of Le Saulchoir. He thanked Gillet 'for the discretion and kindness with which, without sacrificing just firmness, you have alluded to Fr Ch[enu]'.[111] The Roman archives of the Order hold a file for the congratulations Gillet received, although two of these express fear of an alignment on the Angelicum's rigid Thomism. Fr Gerlaud, Regent of Studies at the Lyon Province noted 'how regrettable it would be, because of the impoverishment, for one college, and much less the whole Order, to be fixed on a single yardstick of minds, whether that be the yardstick of the rigid Thomists or of others! The progress of doctrine would compromised if both parties, rather than mutually anathematising each other, did not seek to understand one another and to rectify the extremes of each of their positions.' This prudent formulation might also give the impression that he was turning his back on the Angelicum and Le Saulchoir, but at the time of the sanctions against the latter, this point seemed above all to be made against

---

110. Pages 96–97.
111. Letter dated 9 May 1942, AGOP V 306.

the former, which Gillet had given as an example.[112]
The Belgian François-Marie Braun, professor of New
Testament exegesis at Fribourg university, while taking
refuge behind the Thomist orthodoxy of his master
Lagrange, proposed that 'if the colleges of our provinces
must become the citadels (or fortresses) of our doctrine,
we will sometimes risk suffocating from this. Bringing in
a little foreign air would surely be a remedy', which hardly
went in the direction of the Generalate's prescriptions.[113]
Le Saulchoir was thus not as isolated as it seemed, while
its pretensions might have appeared excessive, those of
the Angelicum were just as worrying at the very hour of
its apparent victory.

4.2. Sanctions

The placing on the Index of Chenu's booklet did however
bring about serious damage for the French Province's
studium. Not only was its Rector removed from his
post and forbidden to teach, but its governing body was
completely replaced by the Holy Office without taking
the regulations of the Dominican order into account.
In addition to Thomas Philippe, who replaced Chenu,
Héris joined, replacing Deman as vice-rector, and Paul
Philippe replaced Spicq as Master of Students. His arrival,
as a former pupil currently working at the Angelicum,
had been announced at the start of the visitation.[114] The
devolving of the leadership of the *studium*'s studies to
two speculative Thomists, fully trusted by Fr Garrigou-
Lagrange, changed its direction profoundly. In addition

---

112. Letter dated 2 April, same source.

113. Letter dated 29 April, same source.

114. 'I am very happy that they are thinking of sending Fr Paul',
as Thomas Philippe wrote to Garrigou-Lagrange on 6 May.

to Chenu, the whole of Le Saulchoir suffered from the 1942 crisis. For further security, the highest authority added that the teaching of theology and philosophy in the three houses of study in French must take place in Latin, although there was nothing of this in the letter from Cardinal Marchetti-Selvaggiani about the *Revue des sciences philosophiques et théologiques*, nor in the first consignment of decisions from Gillet on 10 December 1942. On 26 March 1943 Thomas Philippe clarified that the journal was entrusted to Guérard des Lauriers and would have new censors, but that Chenu could continue to publish in it.[115] Gillet's letter, dated 7 March and received on 24 April, indicated that it was the general editorship of the journal, not its secretariat, which would be transferred from Chenu to Guérard, even though Chenu was not its editor!

4.2.1. Chenu

The Holy Office also clarified that Chenu could not be assigned to the house at boulevard Latour-Maubourg which was home to the Éditions du Cerf. In September 1943, he left Le Saulchoir, to which he had given his best for twenty-three years, never to return. He was assigned to Paris Saint-Jacques, a convent in the Province where he would be 'the least disoriented'.[116] Settling in the working-class heart of the 13th arrondissement of Paris would definitely change the future direction of his journey: already an adviser to various undertakings of mission

---

115. Note quoted by Dewailly.

116. As Fr Faidherbe wrote to him in a card dated 22 April 1942; 'Fr Provincial has sent me my posting', letter to Duval dated 14 August; his posting announced at Le Saulchoir on 12 September according to the house chronicle.

within France, Chenu would give more and more to this, without being part of the Resistance,[117] or abandoning the history of medieval theology.

Just as he was being sanctioned for having sold out Thomism, he completed, in a sort of sad irony, the reworking of his 1927 article on 'La Théologie comme science au XIIIᵉ siècle'. This volume, whose preface is dated March 1942, a month after the Holy Office decree, was to

---

117. This is a blindspot in the rich historiography of the theologian. From a Republican background and hostile to Action Française, he was so unfavourable to the regime change in 1940 that Gillet, with the support of Pétain, asked Motte on 4 October 1940, to advise him to tone down his criticisms. 'I claim responsibility for my freedom all the more as I am scandalised [. . .] to see that, for so many men reported to be strong, *force* and its triumph have become an 'argument' which makes them consider true today what they claimed yesterday was false, and good, what they had said was evil. If force were to sweep it away definitively, I know that many clerics would run behind the new tank; for myself, I would have enough force to imitate Lacordaire when faced with the theologians of the Sainte Alliance', Chenu replied to the Provincial on 5 November. He therefore certainly shared the mindset of the resistance, as is shown three years later by his reservations about the Service du travail obligatoire [the sending of able-bodied Frenchmen to work in Germany]: 'I have hesitated, Fr Ch'nu's advice was categorical, and I held back, as Fr Provincial did not give me a formal order', wrote Fr Jomier to his confrere Anawati, having been asked to accompany those sent to Germany as a voluntary chaplain (Dominique Avon, *Les Frères prêcheurs en Orient*, 440). The psychological shock of the Roman sanction may partly explain why this resistant mind-set did not become participation in the active Resistance. None of the works on spiritual Resistance mention Chenu.

appear in the *'Bibliothèque thomiste'* which he edited on behalf of Librairie Vrin. 'Fr Chenu has just come to put the finishing touches to a complete reworking, much broader, of his earlier study on '"la théologie comme science au XIIIᵉ siècle": a study totally to the glory of St Thomas and speculative theology! When I think of the complaint that he "brings discredit on scholastic theology" and St Thomas too, I think I am dreaming', Motte wrote to Louis on 1 May 1942. The disconnect between this work and the sanction which struck its author appeared striking, as the work of St Thomas was presented in this book as the apogee of medieval theology. In truth, his enemies could find some grist to their mill in it. Henry Donneaud has recently shown convincingly how Chenu's intellectual and religious experience had led him to turn the meaning of his demonstration upside down. In 1927 he sought, not without 'a certain rationalism', to prove that Thomist theology was a science, in the Aristotelian sense of the term.[118] In 1943, he tended to relativise this scientific nature, at the risk of making himself vulnerable to one of the complaints made about him: that Thomist theology was nothing more than an 'imperfect science' partially dependent on the religious atmosphere in which it was developed.[119] The second edition of *La Théologie comme science au XIIIᵉ siècle* thus confirms the decisive development of Chenu's thought since his manifestos of 1935 ('Position de la théologie') and 1937 (*Une école de théologie*). But its author had felt threatened well before being placed on the Index, and so the reworking of his

---

118. Henry Donneaud, 'Histoire d'une histoire. M.-D. Chenu et "la théologie comme science au XIIIᵉ siècle"', in *Mémoire dominicaine,* 4 (Spring 1984): 139–175 at 145.

119. Donneaud, 'Histoire d'une histoire. M.-D. Chenu et "la théologie comme science au XIIIᵉ siècle"', 159.

pioneering article of 1927 sought to be an ironical and sometimes lyrical testimony of 'fervour for Thomism'.[120]

And yet the book needed to be published. Thomas Philippe took seven months to read the book which Motte had placed before him on his arrival at Le Saulchoir. His reaction was generally positive: despite some expressions which needed correcting, 'your manuscript explains the traditional thesis in a most interesting way using historical data', he wrote to Chenu on 11 December 1942.[121] The publication was nevertheless subjected to supervision by the Master General a month and a half later.[122] Chenu, in disagreement with his provincial on this point, rejected the advised procedure: he preferred to bypass the *imprimatur* and publish his work *pro manuscripto*, with a limited run. The volume, dedicated to the memory of the Le Saulchoir masters Gardeil, Mandonnet, and Lemonnyer, included a sadly ironic post-scriptum: 'Fr Chenu brings discredit to scholastic theology, to its speculative nature, its methodology, and the value of the conclusions it draws from the revealed data. And this discredit falls on St Thomas', a statement attributed to Parente (*Osservatore Romano*, 9–10 February 1942), and countersigned by Garrigou-Lagrange and Thomas Philippe, 'apostolic Visitors to Le Saulchoir'. An equally incisive typed slip was added to some volumes: the work

---

120. Donneaud, 'Histoire d'une histoire. M.-D. Chenu et "la théologie comme science au XIIIᵉ siècle"', 170.

121. Fr Chenu was thus wrong to state that 'the Visitor kept the manuscript in a drawer without reading it', personal note inserted into some editions.

122. Letter from Thomas Philippe to Chenu dated 24 January 1943, which suggested alterations for some expressions 'which risk recalling the short work, le Saulchoir une "école de théologie" and your article in the R.S.P.T. of May 1935'.

had already been completed by the censors in May 1942 when a canonical visitor, Fr Th. Philippe, arrived at Le Saulchoir charged with enquiring into the teaching of the Faculties, incriminated in particular for devaluing reason in theology, discrediting scholastic theology and its speculative nature, and thus lessening its value as an academic discipline. The manuscript of the work was handed to the visitor. A work on 'theology as a science' was clearly of major importance to him, the more so as this was the draft of teaching which had been given for twenty years in the theology faculty.

Now he does not seem to have taken account of this.[123] The obstacles placed in the way of his theological career could only strengthen Chenu's inclination to concern himself with 'theological tropes in action', which for him were apostolic and missionary initiatives.

4.2.2. Chenu's Circle

Chenu was not the only one in the hot seat: several of his colleagues had various reasons to be anxious, for the visitors' mandate concerned the whole teaching body at Le Saulchoir. 'Changes in the teaching staff seem to me to be essential so that in October we can start again in the right direction', wrote Thomas Philippe to Garrigou at the start of May 1942. His report on the *studium* thus included a paragraph on each of them, 'in the sense you said to me, whether or not we can keep such-and-such a professor'. Congar and Dubarle, then prisoners of war, raised a delicate problem for their captivity in Germany seemed to be punishment enough without adding

---

123. *La Théologie comme science au XIIIe siècle*, 1943. I consulted Fr André Duval's copy.

another. 'However, I shall try to get some information about them', clarified the visitor.[124]

Congar, known to be in complete solidarity with Chenu, saw his file become larger in 1942. 'I have been told that one of Fr Congar's books has been published in his absence, and I have already heard that in this second book, *not edited by him*, as in the first one, there are ambiguous formulas, which have already found disapproval earlier. Fr Congar was warned by me at the time, and promised me that he will correct these statements and this promise has prevented major trouble. But if he has not been able to personally review the book, why has he published it', wrote Gillet to Motte on 17 May 1942. He was writing about *Esquisses du Mystère de l'Église*, the eighth volume in the '*Unam Sanctam*' series. This collection of various articles and other contributions was published in 1941, with the *imprimatur* dated August.[125] In particular it included writings in which Congar admitted his debt to Johann Adam Möhler, whom Garrigou-Lagrange had complained inspired Chenu. One can understand Gillet's agitation, as he had not received the book,[126] but he was appealing to the provincial's responsibility. But as the book was simply a republication of texts which had already been published with the necessary permissions, the provincial had not thought it wise to subject them to a new examination and had given the green light. In light of the Chenu affair, he realised his mistake and decided

---

124. Letter dated 6-8 May.

125. Final point: 'To the Army, 18 January 1940'; *imprimatur* given in Paris on 22 August following the agreement of Chenu and Motte.

126. Congar sent him two copies in 1945, following his return from Germany (letter dated 11 July, AGOP XIII 30200/2 file 12).

motu proprio to withdraw the book from sale, 'harsh as this decision might appear to our poor Father, held captive for two years, and to the publishers Éditions du Cerf'. In this was he thought he was going beyond the wishes of the Master General and the Holy Office.[127]

However *Esquisses* was not Congar's only work to worry Rome. 'Fr Garrigou-Lagrange [. . .] has written to me about the concerns he anticipates from the article *Théologie* (although he has not read it) for which Fr Congar is responsible', wrote Mgr Amann, editor of the *Dictionnaire de théologie catholique* to his friend Cardinal Tisserant, on 5 June 1942. 'I fear difficulties for this article from a certain side [. . .] it seems it will be dissected in the highest places', he confirmed on 1 July.[128] The first part of the article, which Thomas Philippe had neglected to read,[129] was published without difficulty in a volume in 1943. This echo outside the Dominican world confirmed that everything coming out of the theological school of Le Saulchoir was now under suspicion.

On 4 March 1942, Féret contested what the provincial reproved him of. It was not true that he claimed 'to read and interpret Scripture directly, *without any recourse to dogma nor any support from later theology*', as Motte suspected him of doing. 'The more I study the sources, that is Scripture and the life of the Church, the more I feel at ease reading St Thomas. I would not say the same, it is true, for dialectical theology which in too many

---

127. Letter to Gillet dated 7 May, probably actually 7 June, since Gillet's letter arrived with him on 1 June, ADF, copy.

128. Letters kept among the Tisserant papers, held by the association Les Amis du Cardinal Tisserant, 66150 Montferrer.

129. Personal note inserted into some volumes of *théologie comme science au XIIIe siècle*.

places has supplanted St Thomas' influence', he added, in line with Chenu. What was he to do in these conditions with the manuscript which he had just completed on the Apocalypse, a difficult subject matter, 'without giving rise to the suspicion of 'Evangelism' which you dread!'[130]

Deman, professor of moral theology, and Spicq, professor of New Testament exegesis, experienced lectors who had passed their examination *ad gradus* in January 1936, were candidates for the Master of Sacred Theology. This was requested from Rome by Motte on 28 September 1942, but refused to them, despite the support of the Provincial Chapter in July 1943. Such a refusal was no surprise: how could they be given such a promotion when they had just been removed from the college's governing body? Nonetheless this gave rise to bitterness for the two, Deman in particular, who was at the forefront of resistance to the visitor:[131] 'his attitude, during the change of editor for the Revue des sciences, was entirely unacceptable', Thomas Philippe justified himself before clarifying that the rebel had later returned to the ranks.[132] The terms in which the refusal was couched 'simply as a precaution of prudence' proves that it was less the works of the two religious in question than the general climate of suspicion around the house where they taught.

And yet, aside from the arrival of Paul Philippe and the promotion of Thomas Philippe to the Master of Sacred Theology, required for him to be confirmed in the role of

---

130. The book was published in 1943 by Corréa, with the title *L'Apocalypse de saint Jean. Vision chrétienne de l'histoire*, and gave rise to lively discussion.

131. Letters to Fr dated 8 November 1943 (Deman) and undated (Spicq).

132. Letter to Gillet dated 10 November 1943, AGOP XIII 30200/2 file 12.

Regent, no transfer happened immediately. Deman and Féret were therefore unaware that it had been decided to remove them from Le Saulchoir until they were informed. 'Having weighed everything up', Thomas Philippe wrote to Gillet on 10 November 1943, 'I think that keeping Frs Deman and Féret here is the best decision for the time being'. The two suspects would only learn later that they had avoided leaving Le Saulchoir in 1943. Gillet revealed it to Deman at the time of his transfer to Fribourg in 1945. Fr Féret learned about it from Gillet's successor, Fr Suarez, in March 1947.[133] We do not know the reasons for such a shift, which calmed the local superiors: the house was already troubled enough by Chenu's leaving not to add further to its confusion. But the argument turned again: more brutal sanctions from 1943 onwards would have been a short sharp shock, without allowing suspicions to grow, only ending in February 1954 with the expulsion of Féret and Congar. There were many other professors at Le Saulchoir, but the threats weighing on the lectors close to Fr Chenu prove that it was the entire line he defended which was targeted by the visitation.

4.2.3. Les Éditions du Cerf

The letter from the Holy Office, about measures to be followed, dated 3 November 1942 is as prolix as the information about the visitation to Boulevard Latour-Maubourg is succinct. Fr Gillet must have moved aside Fr Boisselot, the Superior of the convent and director of the Éditions du Cerf, replacing him with Fr Constant Dorange, whose assistant was to be Fr Spitz. The journal *La Vie*

---

133. This matter was document by the then archivist of the French Province, Fr André Duval, and written up at our request (EF).

Intellectuelle was to endeavour to focus more on 'truths of the supernatural order than contemporary temporal problems', while collaboration with lay authors was to be better 'overseen and checked'. To avoid any deviations, censorship would be allotted to Frs Noble and Courtois, with appeal to the Master General in case of difficulty. In addition, it was appropriate that the religious assigned to this apostolate should be sent to Rome to complete their formation. In *La Vie spirituelle*, it was necessary to avoid 'intellectualising the interior life to the point that one might believe such a life is only to be possessed following some study of mystical writings', and above all 'falling into a false spiritualisation of theology by reducing it to a religious experience', which was one of the main misguided ways attributed to Chenu. In order to avoid these dangers, the editorial committee of the journal was to include a competent theologian who would prepare a report twice a year on the articles which were to be or had recently been published. Then, to 'counterbalance and fulfil the influence of "*La Vie intellectuelle*", it would be appropriate for "*La Vie spirituelle*" to remain under the control of the theologians of Le Saulchoir, particularly the Regent of the college', Thomas Philippe. Even before the measure was announced, Chenu was interpreting the threat as the logical outcome of the trouble at Cerf from 1937, with the suppression of *Sept* and the risk that *Vie intellectuelle* would also be suppressed. Chenu wrote to Mgr Beaussart,

> Of course you know that the placing on the Index of my little work is only one small episode in a tornado which is targeting wider objectives, and threatens to bring us back to the wonderful days of integrism . . . We French Dominicans are most in their sight-lines . . . at least since the time when M. Manacorda, in charge of intellectual propaganda

for M[ussolini], led a press campaign against the French "communist Dominicans". It was following that that Le S[aulchoir], where the Roman emissary is working to turn back methodologies and mind-set, and the editorship of the journals (Vie Spir., Vie Int., etc) at the Éditions du Cerf was threatened: the editorial director, Fr B[oisselot] was sacked because of the Visitor Fr Garr[igou]-Lagrange's decision. This decision was based purely on the prejudices of 1937-38, for the recent canonical visitation carried out by his delegate was amicably basic, and concluded without complaints [...] What they want here is not to get rid of such-and-such a person, but to attack a mind-set, on behalf of a doctrinal integrism where there is an opportunity to satisfy the grudges against the V.I. and Fr Bernadot, the bête noire of the A.F. theologians.[134]

As Motte was quick to point out to Gillet,[135] in 1943 this decision had something surrealist about it. *La Vie Intellectuelle* had stopped publication in 1940, and since then Boisselot had hardly dealt with it, leaving its editorship to Maydieu, who, in 1941 had founded the 'Rencontres' series to replace it, a series not mentioned in the initial decision.[136] As Chenu also noted, the measure against laity referred[137] to Henri Guillemin's 'Par notre faute' rather than to the events of the Occupation. Further conclusions from Gillet needed to arrive so that the 'Rencontres' journals might be published. *La Vie spirituelle* would no longer be published in Paris, but

---

134. Draft of letter dated 27 October 1942.

135. Letter dated 5 April 1943, ADF, copy.

136. Étienne Fouilloux, 'La collection "Rencontres" (1941–1944)', in *Jean-Augustin Maydieu, Mémoire dominicaine*, Special Edition II (1998): 73–93.

137. Draft of letter to Mgr Beaussart dated 27 October 1942.

in Lyon, edited by Fr Louvel. In particular Motte was sorry that 'one of our most direct and influential points of contact, a privileged means of religious influence' was being attacked. Louis replied from Rome that there was no reason to suppress 'Rencontres', but that the decisions about Boisselot, Dorange and Spitz were to be put in place immediately. 'Fr General cannot change anything about conclusions which he did not make', but which had been made by the Holy Office.[138] While Boisselot, assigned to the convent of the Annunciation on the rue du faubourg Saint-Honoré, did not lose contact with his Parisian environment, 'the peeling off of Dorange', according to the Archbishop of Rouen, Mgr Petit de Julleville, as reported by Spicq,[139] was not as easy, first of all because Dorange and Spitz, who unlike the priests assigned to the boulevard Latour-Maubourg[140] were not lectors and did not have particular experience in publishing, which Dorange was open about. 'He clearly objected to me that he did not feel able to take on this task, but he would lean on obedience and the divine aid that would ensure', Thomas Philippe wrote to Gillet on 6 April 1943, shortly before the new editorial board was installed on 3 May. Dorange thus wanted to have clear directions about his role, because he wished to exercise 'a real control and effective leadership over the editors of the journals', especially and ultimately because the Éditions du Cerf belonged not to the Dominican Order but to a private company whose majority shareholders were lay people, two of the most influential of whom, 'very attached to the memory of Fr Bernadot', had made their opposition to

---

138. Letter dated 20 April 1943.
139. Undated letter to Fr Chenu.
140. Rome sent the licence for the lectorate for Dorange (Philippe's thank you to Gillet dated 18 May).

the change of editorship very clear. 'These "good lay folk" claim not to want to intervene in questions of doctrine, but say that they have advanced serious capital for such-and-such a work and that they do not want it to change direction', Philippe wrote to Gillet on 18 May. 'Legally they are the owners of Éditions du Cerf', and nothing could be done without them, so it was difficult to find a compromise. The administrative council agreed with regret to Boisselot's removal, but no replacement was appointed. In the meantime, Fr Thomas-George Chifflot took over and continued the work without the job-title. Perhaps later it would be possible to appoint Dorange as editorial director, but for the time being this solution seemed to be 'the only one possible to respond to Rome's wishes and to keep the Société du Cerf in existence', the Visitor conceded.'[141]

4.2.4. The *Revue des sciences*

Roma locuta, causa finita? 'I hope that we will soon have notice of the closing of the apostolic visisitation which will make the situation clearer from a legal perspective', Motte wrote to Rome on 16 April 1943. 'The coup at the R.S.P.T. allows a deep fear to persist that the hydra will grow new heads.'[142] Louis replied on 2 May that there would be no more; but Chenu did not consider the matter closed. At the start of May he wrote a lengthy letter to the Regents and Masters of Sacred Theology of the Order in which he refined his version of the affair. The *Revue des sciences* had not given rise to criticism and had never been in question during the visitation: it was three months after the end

---

141. Letter from Philippe to Gillet confirmed by, among others, a letter from Boisselot to Fr Tunmer dated 19 May 1957.

142. Letter to Louis, ADF, copy.

of the visitations that the visitors had obtained 'the
decision to remove the editorial board . . . to appoint a
single editor, without any consultation with the fraternal
team of collaborators, and to appoint two super-censors.'
Once this was known outside the Order, the measure gave
rise to condemnation. 'At the Institut, three of the most
eminent masters of high culture, MM. Faral, Mazon, and
Picard twice expressed [. . .] their sorrow at seeing the
Church periodically bar the way to good academic work
in this way.'[143] The former Regent emphasised the need
for the Catholic Church to participate in 'the renewal of
methodologies' and 'the new position of problems, from
which currents of thought are forming': this had been the
aim of the *Revue des sciences* since 1907, strengthened
by its 'Thomist base', but it would only be possible to
continue this 'if we do not feel the tenacious suspicion
and animosity of certain censors at every step.'[144] Hence
Vrin's decision, taken in agreement with Gilson, to stop
publishing the journal. Motte, about to leave for Rome,
reacted 'in his usual imperative way, forbidding me "with
all the authority of his role" to send a copy of this letter,'
five copies of which had already been sent.[145] Héris and
Deman warmly approved of its intention and contents.[146]
Chenu obeyed while denying the provincial the right
to represent Le Saulchoir, its 'sufferings', its 'mind-set',

---

143. These were the medievalist Edmond Faral, the Slavic
scholar André Mazon, and the archaeologist and historian
of ancient Greece Charles Picard.

144. Undated draft, difficult to read.

145. Letter from Chenu to Héris dated 12 May, on the letter
received from Motte dated 10 May.

146. Letters dated 11 May (Héris) and 12 May (Deman).

and its 'hopes' in Rome.[147] His 'calm firmness' was now more resistance than unconditional surrender, and this was indeed how it was understood by his superiors: the Master General was opposed to Allo's suggestion that Chenu be thanked for his devotion to Le Saulchoir since 1920, as this would 'have the air of disapproving of the Holy Office's decision'. On the contrary, he demanded a joint letter of submission which was signed by all the professors on 13 May 1943.[148]

Motte returned from Rome convinced of the legitimacy of the Holy Office's intervention for which Charlier's book and its review by Draguet had been merely an opportunity to settle earlier grievances. This was a blow to the whole Order, not only Chenu, and the consequences were not at all exceptional: it was simply a matter of checking the teaching at the *studia*, a task entrusted, 'against his will', to Garrigou-Lagrange. 'It is not the intellectual tradition of Le Saulchoir in itself which has been condemned,' he wrote, 'but only one of its unfortunate manifestations'. A 'siege mentality', and especially 'a certain self-importance' were to be avoided, and provided that all subjectivism and 'excessive indulgence for modern [ideas]' were also removed, serious work might continue, and the house could defend itself against 'deformations' and 'calumnies', he explained to the college on 7 June.[149] He was re-elected

---

147. 'Therefore your intervention can only create yet more confusion in an affair which is already so confused. Do not take on this responsibility', he wrote to him on 12 May before meeting him (letter communicated to Thomas Philippe and to Héris).

148. Copy of Allo's letter to the Master General, undated; letter from Guérard des Lauriers to Chenu dated 14 May; Chenu's thanks to Allo dated 13 July.

149. Note from Dewailly, ADF; see also Héris' account to Chenu dated 9 June.

provincial for four years that July by a chapter which appointed Chenu to be one of the four definitors of the province, an indication that he maintained support there. Strengthened in his authority, Motte no longer disguised his reservations about the Visitor. 'The Province ... has had the painful impression', he wrote that 'Thomas Philippe, afflicted by a conscience which tends to scrupulosity', 'had treated his former masters and colleagues with much severity, and that he remained more of a visitor and outside observer than a Regent dedicated to the interests of his college'.[150]

While he wished to save the *Revue des sciences* 'at any cost', and he had tried before the Provincial Chapter to work for conciliation with Vrin,[151] Motte became painfully aware of the insert Vrin had placed in the second 1941–1942 issue of the *Sciences religieuses*, published in autumn 1943, with a summary which demonstrated the support for the journal in the universities: an editorial by Gilson on 'Le christianisme et la tradition philosophique' and a lengthy article by Gouhier on 'La conversion de Maine de Biran au platonisme'.[152] 'As the editorial committee of the SCIENCES PHILOSOPHIQUES ET THEOLOGIQUES has been changed by orders from on high, the publisher will give up publishing the journal'. 'I think your withdrawal as publisher is disproportionate to the change in the editorial board which you highlight', Motte wrote to Vrin on 2 October. 'I remain convinced that if we want to, we can save the *Revue*, not only materially, but in its essential content and in its own line', just as, according to him, 'the experience of the Éditions du Cerf affected by the same backlash' had shown, and

---

150. Letter to Gillet dated 31 July, copy.
151. Letter of thanks for services, 18 June, copy.
152. Pages 249–66, 267–326.

for which a modus vivendi had been found. But he reckoned the 'open criticism of the Roman intervention' contained in the insert was 'disastrous'. 'Whatever the intrinsic value of the measures taken', they were made by a legitimate authority which had the right to be respected. Divulging information which had remained under the apostolic secret, the protest risked harming the French Dominicans, Chenu in particular, who would be accused of having inspired it. Chenu suggested a compromise solution to Motte to keep the journal going: Guérard would be editorial secretary until Congar's return, not editorial director; the editorial board would remain unchanged; and Héris and Féret would be the two super-censors. But Deman, who had now been refused the Master of Sacred Theology for a second time, even though it had been requested by the Chapter, rejected this compromise. 'The only practice to adopt in this matter is intransigeance . . . in other words, complete passivity', he wrote on 4 November.[153] The plans continued to burn slowly and the matter remained there until Fr Congar's return. Having been unable to break through the enigma of the 1942–1943 sanctions, Congar did not return to this work with great enthusiasm after his lengthy captivity, and the *Revue des sciences philosophiques et théologiques* was only published again in 1947.

---

153. Letter to Chenu.

Conculsion

The Chenu affair is thus close to being fully cleared up. Robert Guelluy's cascade of hypotheses about what happened remains convincing.

> *Une école de théologie* would perhaps not have worried Rome so much if they had not also been preoccupied in 1938 with the boldness of the French Dominican province: the silence on Chenu's booklet would probably not have been broken had Charlier's book, which seemed to continue his ideas in a more public way, not been published; Charlier's book would perhaps not have been condemned had it not been for the resounding review of Draguet, which suggested a large anti-establishment movement bringing the three names, Chenu, Charlier, and Draguet, together.[1]

To move from hypotheses to certainties, we will have to wait for work on the Holy Office archives from the pontificat of Pius XII which are the only ones which can restore the missing link in this plausible sequence

---

1. Guelluey, 'Les antécédents', 478.

between the warnings from Cordovani or Boyer in 1940 and the sanction of 1942.

Chenu and his circle were wrong to see the sanction purely as the response of a 'coterie' devoid of any serious foundation. Not only was Le Saulchoir not the victim of a one-sided cabal, as Chenu implied, but the measures taken against it were not without justification, in form and in content. First of all, the theologians who lined up against Chenu were not only his peers, with whom he could engage in calm debate: through their admission to the Roman dicasteries they tended to confuse their positions with those of the Church's ordinary magisterium, and to behave accordingly. What is more, we should not underestimate the psychological wounds inflicted by Chenu's acidic pen. 'You must see now that I was not wrong when at the start of your Provincialate I drew your attention to what was being said about Le Saulchoir, its claims to run the Order, and its criticism of everyone who . . . did not agree with its views', Master General Gillet wrote to Motte on 7 March 1943.[2] Not only had Chenu scarred some of his Roman conferes – and not the most junior ones – he had also presented Le Saulchoir as a model which looked like an alternative to the formation delivered by the Order's Roman college. Was the dispute reduced to a banal question of jealousy based on misunderstandings, or even ill-will, as the clumsy articles in Parente's officious article might allow us to believe? Or, rather, simply as internal bickering within the 'great family of Thomists', as a new avator of the infamous *rabies theologica*?

The gulf between Le Saulchoir and its detractors has been shown to be wide for other reasons. First of all, there was the conception of the discipline of theology: was it

---

2. Opinion confirmed by his letter dated 13 April.

open to the outside world, or closed in on itself, following Bergson's categories repeated by Aimé Forest in his acknowledgement of receipt of Chenu's brochure?[3] Was it inductive, beginning from 'theological tropes in action' which it singled out, or deductive on the foundation of scholastic formulations of Aristotelian origin, fixed by St Thomas' commentators? Was it purely speculative and abstract, or could it also be 'positive', appealing to the historical-critical method, and with no division between thought and prayer or contemplation? Was it shy about the relativity of its concepts and systems, or certain about its formulations given their closeness to those of the magisterium? Disagreement about methodology in theology, the debate between Le Saulchoir and its detractors was also disagreement about the very subject-matter of theology, that is, the nature of Christian faith. Chenu had touched on this when on 7 March 1942 he had written to Étienne Gilson, 'Revelation as a historical fact', and not as a rational construction, '*this is indeed it*'.[4] Not only should history-with-a-small-h renew the understanding and teaching of theology, but taking History-with-a-captial-H into account profoundly changed its meaning. For Chenu and those close to him, Christian faith was not a coherent collection of doctrines which might be learned by reason alone, but the progressive registering of Revelation in History, simultaneously the history of salvation and the history of humanity in search of salvation. This affirmation of the basic nature of the historicity of the Christian message, in which his enemies wrongly saw a mistake in place of understanding, clearly separates Chenu from his censors. Even though it does not appear so clearly in his polemics,

---

3. Card dated 24 January 1938.
4. Letter dated 7 March.

this was what was ultimately at stake in the crisis of 1942, hence the recurrent accusations of Modernism or semi-Modernism made against him, since the Modernist crisis had already been formed on the relationship between history, theology, and dogma.

While the methods of Chenu's condemnation, and the underlying reasons are still partly obscured, the same cannot be said of the consequences. Immediately, the sanction had few reverberations—and how could it have been otherwise in a France and in a Church which had other things to worry about than a quarrel among theologians. The war had in any case led to the death of many publications which might have been put forward. Gillet thought the matter sufficiently serious that on 13 November 1942 he wrote an encyclical letter reminding anyone in the Order who might have forgotten of the need to teach St Thomas Aquinas' positions: a balanced but firm reminder to the Thomist order, this hardly had an effect either, given the circumstances. The placing on the Index of *Une école de théologie* had been followed by a visitation in which Garrigou-Lagrange was pulling the strings, and which led to a purge both at Le Saulchoir and in the French Dominican Province. Not only did Chenu have to leave as Regent of Studies, but the governing body of the college was completely replaced, and several of those faithful to the old regime were threatened with dismissal. Deman and Spicq, who had not obtained their Master of Sacred Theology, were more affected from the end of the war. Congar and Féret did not know they were on borrowed time, and from this perspective their removal during the purge of February 1954 was simply the completion of the 1943–43 purge. The *Revue des sciences philosophiques et théologiques* had been suppressed by a 'front of rejection' which brought Chenu and Gilson together with the publishers, Vrin, and its future was in the balance. The editorial board at the Éditions du Cerf was profoundly changed, with the removal of Fr Boisselot and the close observation of the journals. From the decree of February 1942, there had been a gradual bringing to heel of the French Province's institution of formation and intellectual means of publication, under threat since 1937.

Yet immediately, and despite Chenu's personal submission, the circumstances and consequences of the visitation gave rise at Le Saulchoir to ill-feeling which, over the question of the *Revue des sciences*, changed into open resistance. Informed of this by Thomas Philippe, Master General Gillet increased ever more urgent calls to obedience to Motte. For Gillet, Le Saulchoir was doubly at fault, guilty of both intellectual pride and doctrinal laxity. The tirades from Rome did not spare the provincial, who put the measures imposed into practice while defending those under him from the charge of non-submission and defending himself from weakness towards them.[5] The war fixed these positions without resolving the problem, which was the same in 1945. 'Fr Thomas Philippe hardly has the trust of the whole college', Gillet wrote to Héris, the unfortunate vice-rector, on 4 August. 'He does not seem especially qualified to take on and coordinate the return to the common work of the journals and of all our intellectual apostolate.'[6]

The consequences of this affair thus went way beyond the case of *Une école de théologie*. Through Chenu's manifesto, Le Saulchoir and what it represented in the Order was sanctioned: the incarnation of the bold reformists of the French Province whose example posed a risk of contagion. The complaints against *Une école de théologie* in 1942 were essentially the same as those in

---

5. Letter to Gillet dated 26 April 1943, ADF, copy.
6. AGOP XIII 30200/2 file 12.

1938, which prevented the Roman Dominicans from being implicated in any way in the sanctioning: it was almost certainly not them who had taken the matter to the Holy Office, but it was their early criticisms which had helped to justify the placing on the Index. By keeping its distance from the speculative theology which had acted as a rampart against Modernism, the historical and inductive methodology practised at Le Saulchoir under Chenu's leadership, well illustrated by the early volumes of the '*Unam Sanctam*' series, risked bringing back an inadmissible neo-Modernism. The accusation, which did not excuse, would be made between 1946 and 1951 against the Jesuit scholasticate of La Fourvière, and once again in 1954 against Le Saulchoir and those close to it. In a certain way, and despite the specific adventures, many of which remain in the shadow, this 1942 affair did indeed cast the die for the recurrent difficulties with Rome experienced by the most innovative sections of French theology until the dawn of the 1960s.